Managing for Learning

A handbook for the personal development
of secondary school teachers and for use
in their initial and in-service training.

Related titles from Macmillan:

Assessment: From Principles to Action
Robin Lloyd-Jones and Elizabeth Bray

In preparation:

Assessing and Teaching Language: Literacy and Oracy in Schools
Mary Neville

Action Research in the Classroom
Jean McNiff

The Caring Role of the Primary School
Editors: Kenneth David and Tony Charlton

Managing for Learning

A handbook for the personal development
of secondary school teachers and for use
in their initial and in-service training.

John Buckley and
David Styan

**MACMILLAN
EDUCATION**

First published 1988

Published by
MACMILLAN EDUCATION LTD
Houndmills, Basingstoke, Hampshire RG21 2XS
and London
Companies and representatives
throughout the world

Printed in Hong Kong

British Library Cataloguing in Publication Data
Buckley, John, 1923
    Managing for learning: a handbook for
    the personal development of secondary
    school teachers, and for use in their
    initial and inservice training.
    1. High schools—Great Britain—
    Administration
    I. Title   II. Styan, David
    373.12′00941

    ISBN 0—333—44588—0

The characters in these case studies are entirely fictional, and
any resemblance to real cases is totally unintentional.

To Carolyn and Mary

To Carolyn and Mark

Contents

Acknowledgements

We are indebted to many colleagues and students who have knowingly or otherwise contributed to this book. It is somewhat invidious to mention individuals, but our special thanks are due to the following:

Barbara Bardsley, Harold Barry, Tony Cassidy, John Taylor and Fred Tye, for their professional advice and encouragement.

The students of many schools, but in particular those of Bredbury Comprehensive School and Marple Ridge High School, Stockport.

John Aldridge and Miranda Carter for their help in preparing text for publication.

Our secretaries Barbara Card and Joan White for their help in the preparation of the manuscript.

We wish to add that the opinions expressed here are our own and not necessarily those of the people who have helped us.

Chapter 1

Management and Schools

There is now a general recognition that schools need to be managed, and many senior staff in secondary schools have received training in management. The need for such training and the recognition that it should be coordinated nationally led to the establishment of the National Development Centre for School Management Training in Bristol. This government initiative took place in 1983 and was accompanied by the provision of specific grants to fund training schemes in management for Heads and other senior staff in primary and secondary schools. Priority was given to the development of basic courses of twenty days' duration and also one term training opportunities.

What has not been recognised is that management training needs to be provided for all those who are responsible for the learning process. Learning, if it is to be effective, needs to be managed. Thus, all teachers are managers.

When management techniques from industry and commerce were first applied to secondary schools, teachers were sceptical and even suspicious. Much of the theory was concerned with structures and organisation and was often expressed in unfamiliar and unacceptable jargon. Teachers saw teaching and learning as a relationship between the teacher and the taught. Such relationships were organic. Some developed and some didn't, but it couldn't be guaranteed that learning would happen simply by establishing organisations and setting up structures. Even when the 'human relations' school of management came along, teachers still did not see it as relevant to teaching or learning. That particular relationship of being 'good with young people' was different. The result was that a gap developed in secondary schools between the senior staff who managed and the 'assistant' teachers who were managed. Originally in the early 1970s the managers were Heads and Deputy Heads, but in the mid- and late 1970s the need began to be expressed for training in middle management, in particular for heads of subject departments and for those holding the so-called 'pastoral' responsibilities for year groups or for houses. The divide was thus shifted to separate senior and middle management from the rest, even though the middle managers spent most of their time teaching. This hierarchy was further emphasised by the salary scales. Class teachers were not recognised as managers because teaching was not recognised as a managerial activity. This exclusion of a large body of the teaching profession from the management of schools has been harmful in that it has weakened school management and reduced the effectiveness of teaching and learning.

Contemporary needs

It is our belief that many teachers do now feel a need for management training and indeed have a considerable appetite for acquiring management skills. They express these needs when asked to indicate areas in which in-service training should be provided. This book is intended to provide such teachers with a rationale for being considered as managers, and with an opportunity to examine management problems throughout the secondary school.

We begin with a simple definition that management is about getting things done by, through and with other people. For example, a good Head organises and operates a school timetable, arranges for effective reporting to parents and assesses the effectiveness of a team of teachers. Equally, a good teacher is effective if children learn. This process involves preparation, organisation, the motivation of children and the assessment of their progress. All these activities are, in our view, managerial. Furthermore, we consider that they are the most important things which happen in a school. It is specifically to carry out these activities that schools exist. Thus teachers share a common professionalism of being first and foremost managers who spend the major part of their professional lives in classrooms, in laboratories, in workshops or in gymnasia. While learning may happen in more informal settings, in playgrounds, on field trips or on excursions to theatres or foreign countries, nevertheless the main thrust of the school's activities appears in the school's timetable of formal lessons. Other activities such as staff meetings, working parties or committees are peripheral to their main occupation of teaching children. It is not unreasonable for teachers to expect these peripheral activities to contribute to the solution of classroom problems, to help them to teach more effectively and to facilitate children's learning. Many of the suspicions of management which arose in secondary schools may have originated in the proliferation of jobs which were termed managerial but which did not seem to relate to the business of teaching and learning. For this reason we begin at what may appear to be the wrong end. Management is generally thought to begin at the top, namely with the Head. Our approach begins with the class teacher. We look up through the school organisation rather than down, examining contemporary needs if schools are to become more effective at their major task of teaching and learning.

Contemporary concerns

In the time which has elapsed since the speech at Ruskin College, Oxford, delivered by the then Prime Minister, James Callaghan, in October 1976 a number of significant changes have taken place which have affected the management of secondary schools. Placing the content and quality of schooling on the political agenda was itself a major change. Emphasis shifted from the external organisation of schools to their internal organisation and to the curriculum. Public concern was now expressed about what was taught in schools and how it was taught. A succession of documents from the government commencing with *Curriculum 11-16* (D.E.S., 1977) urged teachers to examine the content of their curriculum. *The Practical Curriculum*, published by the Schools Council in 1981, stressed the need to examine curricular processes or how the curriculum was taught. Later, *The Curriculum from 5 to 16* (D.E.S., 1985) arose from a speech by the then Secretary of State declaring the government's intention to seek broad agreement about the objectives of the 5 to 16 curriculum. This booklet emphasised the importance of not only what is taught but of how it is taught.

Teaching and learning styles strongly influence the curriculum in practice and cannot be separated from it. (p.7)

These expressions of national concern for the quality of what was going on in classrooms have led to much appraisal by teachers of their own professional practices. One major national exercise involving 41 schools in five Local Education Authorities led to the publication of *Curriculum 11-16. Towards a statement of entitlement. Curriculum reappraisal in action*. (H.M.S.O., 1983).

Alongside this enquiry into the curriculum a concern for school review or school self-evaluation has also developed. This is a means whereby a school examines not only its curriculum but its priorities, organisation and practices by using a checklist of questions which are responded to by all the teachers. The first published example of this process was devised by the ILEA inspectorate and entitled *Keeping the school under review* (ILEA, 1977). Introducing this booklet Guy Rogers wrote:

> The process of self-appraisal, of looking at what you are doing, why you are doing it, whether you are doing it well, whether you ought to be doing something different, is or should be a continuing one in every school.

This process was further examined in the Schools Council project entitled 'Guidelines for Review and Institutional Development in Schools' (GRIDS) which was designed to assist schools in planning for the future and implementing change. It may be seen as applying to schools some of the principles of organisational development, in particular that social institutions facing changes need to involve all their staff in planning and implementing those changes. All the participants need to own the problems and own the solutions if changes are to be effective. Changing schools is a very difficult task and all the teachers need to be involved in this process of identifying problems, establishing priorities and planning for the future.

Junior Management

This book addresses itself to the two contemporary concerns outlined above, namely the concern with effective teaching and learning and the development of strategies for bringing about changes in schools, which involve all the teachers and not just the so-called top and middle management. We take a holistic view of school management. All teachers are managers and not only do they manage at middle and senior levels, but also at a level which we call junior management. Further evidence of a trend towards an acceptance of this notion of junior management may be seen in the developing of a 'main professional grade' as a basis for the defining and rewarding of teachers. Such a concept accepts that teaching is the teacher's major professional task and this may involve the ordering of books, equipment and teaching materials, the planning of courses for students and being responsible for the work of others. This is a clear recognition and inclusion of managerial tasks in the class teacher's job specification.

Future management structures

The recognition that all teaches are managers and share a common professionalism, coupled with the conviction that all teachers in a school should be involved in identifying, planning and implementing changes, raises further questions concerning the management structures which are appropriate for schools now and in the future. An accelerating rate of change is becoming a feature of contemporary life, whether it be in the economic and industrial areas with the continuous influence of technology or in social life modified by changing mores. Schools cannot ignore information technology, patterns of unemployment, the multi-cultural society or the drug cultures. They require management structures which facilitate and do not inhibit responses to these changes. There is considerable doubt whether those management structures which may be described as autocratic or bureaucratic, with steep hierarchies and tight role definitions, possess the flexibility and openness to perform this function. While there are those who would argue that rapid change, central control and political direction create the need for more instant decision making and for an in-line management structure where senior management hands down directives to subordinates, nevertheless we do not consider this to be an appropriate model for the profession of teaching. We therefore offer examples of an alternative participative system of management of which we have direct experience in Britain and in other European countries where much shallower hierarchies exist. The advent of the main professional grade may further foster the development of shallower hierarchies in this country and lead to participative and collegiate systems in which a forum exists for all teachers to influence, if they wish, all the major decisions in a school and in which the senior management fulfils an executive role.

The final chapters of this book treat these issues which we do not believe can be ignored as schools face the premature arrival of the future.

The structure of the book

This is a book designed for all grades of teachers in training, namely those in initial training and those in in-service training. It is suitable for those following B.Ed or P.G.C.E. courses as an introduction to the skills of junior management and as a means of lifting levels of awareness concerning the problems of middle and senior management in secondary schools. It is also appropriate for those studying for a Diploma in School Management or a similar qualification. Advisers, inspectors or lecturers developing courses in school management may wish to use such a work-book as a text or to select from it case studies or exercises when planning their programmes. Teachers in schools who have a responsibility for organising school-based in-service training may find it useful. For schools embarking on whole school review and future planning the book may serve as an introduction, before tackling their own management problems.

The format of the book has two main elements, and is based on material and methods which we have used in our work with teachers and which have been found to work in practice.

1. The case studies provide incidents from school life and are a useful way of opening up discussion. We begin with young teachers in their first job, somewhat bewildered by an experience for which their initial training has left them only partially prepared. They learn to cope, acquire skills for survival and become more effective junior managers. A further series of incidents illustrates the needs and problems of teachers which can be met by middle managers, not only the ordering of books and the preparing of syllabuses, but providing support, encouragement, counselling and assessment – leading a team. Senior management is treated in the same way, from the point of view of those whom they manage, bringing stability and discipline to a school, providing resources, and introducing new ideas, but not so many as to disturb the stability too often. The case studies raise a wide variety of issues involving management, such as classroom practice, meetings, resources, delegation, discipline, organisation, staff appraisal and structures for decision making. Running through all are the themes of human relationships. Case studies provide common ground when teachers are brought together from a number of schools and are distanced from the immediate experience of the teachers' own

schools which may be too threatening or at least too close for
comfort. Principles can be drawn out of case studies which may be
applied in the teacher's own situation. Questions for discussion
and project work follow the case studies. Their use is examined
more fully in the following chapter.

2. The chapters of continuous text develop a coherent theme and
    present a personal and subjective view of managing schools. Our
    conclusions are practical rather than theorectical because they
    spring from a practical rather than an academic background. They
    are not based upon research findings but upon personal
    experience of working in schools and working with teachers on
    courses in school management. We respect the role of researchers,
    but simply claim that experienced practitioners have a perspective
    which may illuminate the running of schools just as research in its
    own way may provide illumination. These chapters are in no way
    intended to provide answers or solutions to the issues raised in the
    case studies. They should be seen as a commentary, both
    stimulating and provocative, which serves to initiate further
    discussion and leads to further study. At the end of each of these
    chapters a number of references are provided for this purpose.

    This book challenges the traditional view of school
management, examines real school situations and invites their
analysis. It offers a coherent approach to managing schools which
enhances the role of those who teach children, giving them a status
which in our view, is long overdue.

References

D.E.S. (1977) *Curriculum 11-16* (London, H.M.S.O.).
D.E.S. (1983) *Curriculum 11-16. Towards a statement of entitlement.
Curriculum reappraisal in action.* (London, H.M.S.O.).
D.E.S. (1985) *The Curriculum from 5-16. Curriculum Matters 2.* (London,
H.M.S.O.)
ILEA (1977)*Keeping the school under review* (London, Inner London
Education Authority).
THE SCHOOLS COUNCIL (1981) *The Practical Curriculum. Working
Paper 70.* (London, Methuen Educational).

Chapter 2

The Scope and Variety of Management Training for Schools

How to use this book

This book is designed to help those who are learning to manage children's learning more effectively. The learners in this case are teachers who are adults. It is ironic that in education more is known about the way children learn than about the way their teachers learn. We have been involved in working with teachers over many years, have a combined experience as Heads of secondary schools of over twenty years and a lengthy experience of planning training programmes in school management, yet we would be the first to recognise that there is little certainty about the behaviour and motivation of teachers in a learning situation. The empirical evidence on the developmental psychology of adults is not impressive. There is little agreement about the most effective methods of teaching them.

If one of the aims of management training is to lift levels of awareness, then providing information for cognitive learning may suffice. However, our experience convinces us that such training must achieve much more if it is to be effective in changing attitudes, modifying behaviour and equipping the learners with management skills. A wide range of teaching methods is necessary and one purpose of this book is to offer a range of alternative activities.

Many difficulties and uncertainties face those who are called upon to plan and develop programmes in school management, particularly if they are not working full time in the training field. Many of those at present involved in producing and operating course programmes already have full-time jobs which subject them to considerable pressure and involve day-to-day problems of crisis management. They include the Heads and senior staff of schools, L.E.A. advisers and inspectors, and members of H.M. Inspectorate. As course directors they do not often have time to produce teaching materials or to think and talk through their use in practice. As a result course programmes may be hurriedly put together and inadequately prepared. When we were working at a regional management centre it was our habit to precede all course sessions by a full day's preparation and briefing at which the directorate worked closely with the part-time consultant course tutors, all practising Heads, at preparing and rehearsing all the materials which were subsequently to be used. The importance of these planning sessions cannot be overestimated and our first recommendation to all course directors is to devote adequate time and care to the preparation of teaching materials and the composition and timing of sessions which go to make up a course programme. It will prove to be time well spent.

The second result of hasty and inadequate planning is the temptation to produce a programme of the lecture seminar type often composed of a series of lectures followed by plenary discussion and questions and subsequently by discussion in groups. While recognising the value of lectures which may provide information or inspiration, we do not consider they can form the major teaching method employed in management training. The content of such training includes skills of motivation, problem solving, consultation, decision making and the resolving of conflicts. These skills all come within the field of human relationships and are notoriously difficult to teach. Nevertheless, they are more likely to be acquired by a methodology which involves practice followed by feedback on performance and are unlikely to be learned only by cognitive means. Mintzberg (1975) expressed clearly this challenge to the trainers of managers:

> Cognitive learning is detached and informational, like reading a book or listening to a lecture. It is necessary but cognitive learning no more makes a manager than it does a swimmer. The latter will drown the first time he jumps into the water, if the coach never takes him out of the lecture hall, gets him wet, and gives him feedback on his performance. (p.61)

We ourselves have faced the very real difficulties which confront the providers of school management training in both programme preparation and course content. In the absence of any well-established and generally accepted method we offer suggestions which come directly from our experience and which we hope will help those who face similar difficult tasks. Training methods are beginning to change radically and the traditional approach through lectures and seminars is coming under critical scrutiny, while alternative methods have yet to be evaluated thoroughly and authenticated. It is recognised that this method does not ensure that learning is transferred into action. We need to employ a wider variety of teaching methods and teaching materials if we are to hope to change attitudes and beliefs and if these are to be converted into behaviour and action. This work-book aims to provide a number of the alternatives which we have found to be effective.

We go a stage further to assert that to be ultimately effective management training must act directly upon the individual teacher's own school. Some activities must relate directly to the school situation. For example, analysis might be carried out of current practices in teaching a subject by a teacher or a team of teachers. A similar analysis could be made of current decision-making processes by a Head or by a senior mangement team. In either case plans to introduce change could be formulated and implemented during the period of training, with support and consultative help being provided by the trainers. A significant aim of this book is to provide exercises which serve as 'bridges' to that fundamentally important stage when an adult learner applies management skills to change or modify aspects of his or her own school.

Theory and practice

It is our experience that many teachers are suspicious of theory and of those who come from a purely academic background. They favour a methodology which relates to practice in schools. Hence the approach we take is to begin with the known and the familiar, to start with case studies presenting real situations to which teachers can relate. This preference for the practical is expressed succinctly by a teacher commenting on management training in Northern Ireland.

> The abstract discussion of theoretical issues must not predominate. Discussion must focus on practical issues . . . Discussion should move from the concrete to the abstract, not from the abstract to the nebulous. (O'Shea, 1983) (p.32)

We recommend starting with practical examples before proceeding to draw out principles and philosophy, which can then be applied in a learner's own situation. The teacher's suspicion of the academic does, however, in our experience, present the trainer with a dilemma because there is a danger that training may lose its academic rigour and degenerate into providing practical tips and instant answers to problems which teachers have brought with them from their schools. For this reason we offer suggestions for further reading at the end of each passage of text in which we have commented on the practical issues raised in the case studies. As we have stated earlier, research findings are very relevant and must contribute to any serious study. Teachers do not, however, find them an appropriate point of departure for tackling school management problems.

Case studies

The case studies in this book are drawn from our own experiences and illustrate incidents in daily school life. Many of them have already been used in management courses with teachers and they have proved a useful and popular basis for discussion. An important requirement is their credibility, and they prompt a ready response from teachers when they represent a genuine picture of what life is like in schools. We have often used them to begin a course, rather than starting with a lead lecture by a prestigious speaker, simply to give credibility to the course and to establish the credentials of the course providers.

Case studies are used to introduce topics which are to be discussed or studied further. They are presented in a variety of formats, either as continuous narratives or as documents which might appear in an in-tray. They are not too long and do not include too wide a spectrum of issues as this makes it more difficult for a group discussion to focus on the key topics. The quality of discussion arising out of a case study will depend upon many factors, among which the quality of the group leader is undoubtedly of major importance. An average session to read and discuss each of the case studies in this book should take about one and a half hours. There is no copyright restricting the use of these case studies and they may be copied for use in training sessions.

Commentaries

After each set of case studies which deals with a particular aspect of management there is a commentary. The commentaries taken together provide a coherent approach to managing schools. They will be useful to individuals who are pursuing private study and to groups which are following a course of study. The commentaries are related closely to their respective case studies, from which they draw examples and on which they make observations.

For individuals the intention is to provide a perspective which will provoke thinking and encourage further study. The commentaries are followed by suggestions for further study.

The commentaries may also be used by groups as a basis for discussion either separately or side-by-side with the case studies. In an individual school in which in-service management training is being undertaken the commentaries may serve as preliminary papers to introduce a topic or initiate discussion, before tackling a specific problem within the school or before embarking on some form of school review. They have a valuable function as a 'bridge' between opening up the study of a problem in a neutral context and focusing specifically on that problem in the school so that training may be brought to bear directly upon it.

The commentaries also provide some indication of the content and curriculum for management training at the level concerned and some suggestions as to methods which might be used. These will be helpful for those planning programmes for school management training and are based upon our experience of providing such training.

Group discussion and other group activities

In our experience there is no doubt that the training activity most widely appreciated by participants in management training is the group discussion. In a small group members have the opportunity to air their views and share their experiences in an atmosphere that is less threatening than in a large plenary session. Group size is important and the optimum size appears to be no fewer than five and no more than ten members, the most commonly favoured size being seven or eight members. Such groups develop their own 'climate', ethos or atmosphere and can produce a cohesiveness which often lasts long after the training period is over. It is our experience that the group discussion is a potent environment for learning and provides a close relationship with professional colleagues which builds confidence and shares anxieties in an atmosphere which is supportive and helpful. This valuable element of group discussions may also be comfortable and rather remote from the real world of schools. One must remain aware that what people say in a group will not necessarily be translated into practice and action in a school. Discussion in the 'ivory tower' of the seminar room will not guarantee that schools are managed better. Nevertheless, group discussion does play an important part in school management training and we provide many examples of topics for such discussions.

Once again it must be stressed that the quality of a discussion will depend on the qualities of all the participants, and above all will depend upon the quality of the group leader. While it is not our intention to provide a detailed study of the function of small groups, it may be helpful to indicate some of the attributes which go to make an effective group leader. Note that we deliberately use the term 'leader'. We do not favour a 'neutral' chairman or an *ad hoc* decision by a group to select its own chairman; the role of group leader is a demanding one and requires careful preparation beforehand. Nor do we favour a style of group leadership which is dominant or directive as this merely inhibits discussion and frustrates those with contributions to make. Group leadership requires sophisticated skills to be exercised in a way which is consistent and predictable, providing sufficient control to ensure participation by all members of the group. Discussion should not be allowed to range so widely as to be diffuse and should not be so tightly structured as to inhibit useful contributors. The shy member may need to be prompted and drawn into the discussion, the garrulous and insensitive may need to be restrained. Group leaders need highly developed skills of human interaction, notably a sensitivity to group atmosphere and an understanding of the mental and social processes going on in a group. It is our belief that the role of group leadership in this sense is one which requires training.

Discussion is not, of course, the only activity in school management training which takes place in groups. A number of workshop exercises and projects are provided in this book as group activities. Most such exercises aim to produce an end result. The group is asked to compose over a given period some form of written report or to offer a presentation of their findings to other groups or to all the members of a course. The presentation is often accompanied by documentation or by illustrations on transparencies for an overhead projector. Again, as with case studies, we have found such exercises very effective as long as they are credible and genuinely relate to school life. We have known them engage the interest of a group over a substantial period and for group members to devote more time and energy to the exercise than originally intended by the trainers.

More elaborate simulation exercises do not come within the scope
of this book, but may be briefly mentioned as group activities which
have enjoyed a considerable vogue. It is our view that these exercises
may be successful but increasingly they are being replaced in training
programmes by the study of real rather than imaginary situations. To
be successful, simulation exercises need to be prepared with the
greatest care and in the fullest detail. Those with which we have been
associated have used a variety of media. An exercise of this nature may
require a small production team of, say, three or four persons with
particular skills in writing, drama and technology. The materials
produced to present a school situation might include maps, video-
taped sequences, a slide and tape presentation, role play and a wide
variety of background material and documentation. All this might
take some months to prepare, require creativity and imagination, plus
a firm grip on reality.

Role play

Role play is a training method widely used in programmes in which
personal awareness and social processes are being explored. Again we
do not propose to examine the psychological or sociological
justification for this type of activity but simply to report on our
experience of using it with teachers. Role play generally appeals more
to younger teachers than to their older and more senior colleagues.
Many senior teachers are often highly sceptical of this type of exercise
unless it has been very carefully structured and unless the scenario has
been composed with the maximum attention to realism. When the
roles of the participants have been drawn with skill and insight into
attitudes and human behaviour they may provoke a lively interest,
and a learning situation may develop. The skill seems to lie in
providing the participants with enough information to create a real
situation, but not so much as to swamp them with too much
preliminary reading matter. It is also crucial for the trainers to
demonstrate that they are closely in touch with the day-to-day life of
schools otherwise the exercise may invite criticism or even ridicule.

Future developments in management training

The acceptance of the notion that the career development of all
teachers should include an element of annual in-service training is

leading to the expansion of course provision for teachers at all grades. Management training has been selected as one of those areas which should receive specific government funding (GRIST). The case studies, questions for discussion, in-service projects and commentaries in this work-book are offered within this context. The material may be used by an individual student for personal study. It may also be used by the whole staff of a school for an in-service course or by faculty or year teams within a school for a similar purpose. Individual case studies or other exercises may be selected and copied for distribution to course members. Either case studies or exercises may also serve as models for a school to develop training materials adapted for its own specific needs. The variety of different types of training material offered make it particularly appropriate for short courses in which the members are drawn from a number of schools. In this case variety of material is itself an advantage when composing a programme and the case studies provide common ground on which participants from different schools can meet. This will help to reduce, if not entirely eliminate, the tendency for participants to engage in tedious anecdotes about what happens in their schools. Course directors are provided with authentic material which they may not have the time or the experience to produce themselves.

A further factor in the career development of teachers is the move towards the appraisal of their performance as both teachers and managers. If such appraisal is to play a part in the development of a teacher's career we would prefer that their managerial competence was seen as a major criterion for appraisal. The preparation of lessons, the motivation of children, the development of effective discipline and the assessment of children's work are all aspects of junior management which are worthy of appraisal. Team leadership, preparing syllabuses and schemes of work, conducting meetings and counselling all feature in the role of a middle manager. Communication, negotiation, curriculum development, resource provision, developing structures for consultation and decision making, external relations and managing change are all major aspects of senior management.

These are some of the topics which are treated in the following pages and which should be included in any expanded scheme of in-service and school-focused management training. It is our belief that such training programmes will form an inherent part of the career-long development of teachers. If such training is provided at regular intervals, not for just the enthusiastic few but for all teachers, it can make a major contribution to the professionalism of the teaching service and sustain a continued improvement in the quality of our children's learning.

References

MINTZBERG, H. (1975) 'The manager's job: folklore and fact' in *Harvard Business Review*, 53, 4.
O'SHEA, A.T. (1983) *Management in Secondary Education: An evaluation of the Department of Education's programme of training in educational management for principals of post-primary schools in Northern Ireland* (Belfast, Northern Ireland Council for Education Research).

Chapter 3

Case Studies: First Experiences of a Young Teacher

1. September: a first staff meeting

I parked the car in the playground, empty except for the cars belonging to other teachers, and entered the school building which felt empty too. The corridor had a hollow ring about it. I made my way to the staffroom, peering through classroom doors as I went. The tables and desks were in orderly rows, the blackboards clean, the noticeboards bare. It was the day before school started, and I was taking up my first job as a teacher. I felt very new and did not know quite what to expect. I wondered whether I would be able to cope tomorrow when the building was full of children.

When I arrived in the staffroom, my feelings of anxiety remained. The scene was rather confused and at first I did not recognise anybody. Teachers were busy at lockers or were sorting through brown envelopes which had accumulated in pigeon-holes during the summer holidays. Others were standing or sitting about in groups, engaged in conversation. I looked around for a familiar face, someone I had met on my previous visits to the school. I spotted the Head and wondered whether to go up and speak to her. I knew her as well as anyone after my interview but decided against such an approach. Then, I saw my head of faculty, less recognisable today in his jeans and sweater than when we had last met. He was in earnest conversation with a group of other teachers. I edged my way over towards them and caught his eye. He was immediately welcoming, although somewhat preoccupied with the fact that some examination books had not arrived. He introduced me to other members of the faculty, some of whom I had already met. One actually remembered me, but they all greeted me cheerily and made jocular enquiries as to how I was feeling and whether I was ready for the fray. I smiled and made some appropriate comments. I began to feel better and not quite so isolated. I remained near this group and although I did not follow the 'in' jokes or appreciate the jibes passing to and fro, I began to feel that I belonged to the place.

It all bore little relationship to the day of the interview when I had been the centre of attention, closely shepherded about, plied with coffee and questioned about my ideas and my training. On that day the calm and efficient school secretary had seemed to anticipate my needs. The Head herself had been anxious to tell me about the school and to ask my opinions and impressions of it. Even the caretaker was keen to see that I did not get lost. The day ended with congratulations and the eagerness of everyone to welcome me to the school in September. I had spent another day in the school towards the end of the summer term; many children had left, others were out of school on visits, large numbers seemed to be involved in sporting activities and the school had a relaxed holiday atmosphere about it. Staff whose examination commitments were over had time to sit and chat. I had collected syllabuses and text books feeling very professional and serious. The calm of that day had only been disturbed once by a figure who erupted into the staffroom at breaktime complaining that his fourth-year group had not left (at least not officially). Those who remained did not seem in great demand by staff organising either visits to local factories or tours of stately homes or by those organising sporting activities. However, this incident was quickly forgotten in the general atmosphere of sun and summer. I left the school with a pleasant feeling of euphoria, no longer a student but a trained teacher and, unlike some of my contemporaries, with a real job in a real school. The holidays stretched ahead.

All that seemed a far cry from the hectic scene that faced me now, and little that had happened had prepared me for today, and even more so, for tomorrow. I did not ask the questions that I had wanted to ask. What should I wear? Where did we get our lunch? Who would give me a timetable? What about lists of children? Above all, whom should I ask if I did not know what to do? It was important that I did not look as helpless and as ignorant as I felt. It was important to give a good impression as this was the professional world in which I was going to spend most of my time in the forseeable future. The staff handbook did not help very much with its complicated routines for organising a school visit, for requisitioning stock and for booking audio-visual equipment – these matters seemed of little importance compared with questions which needed urgent answers, such as where I should sit for the meeting, and whether I should take notes.

The members of my faculty were deeply engrossed in discussing the composition of sets and the examination results while other snatches of conversation intruded from colleagues who talked of camping holidays, villas and caravans. These conversations were interrupted by the shuffling of chairs and the movement of people which suggested that the staff meeting was about to begin. I slipped inconspicuously into a chair amongst the members of the faculty as the Head entered carrying a sheaf of papers. After some introductory remarks in which she welcomed us to a new term of a new school year, she went on to address the meeting on a wide range of matters. Other teachers spoke from time to time. Some of their names were whispered to me along with the titles – head of the second year, Mr Stokes; Deputy Head, Mrs James; head of the sixth form, Mr Dowding. Their titles seemed impressive but I had little or no idea of what they actually did. They seemed remote from my concerns which were much more immediate. There was a moment of acute embarrassment when the names of staff new to the school were read out and I had to stand up to be seen by all and recognised. The saga of how the school was coping with the shortage of money continued. The decorations of the science laboratories would not now take place, but it was hoped that the parents would raise some funds for additional computers. Apparently, the public examination results had been better than expected and there were some congratulations for particular faculties. Everyone looked suitably solemn and some exhortations followed concerning the challenges of the new year. Then the meeting was suddenly all over, the Head swept up her papers and there was a mad scramble for lunch at the pub.

Wedged in a corner of the bar I found myself near another newcomer. We made conversation, cautiously, gradually revealing our lack of understanding of what was happening, our joint anxiety about the following day and our apprehensions about the classes which awaited us. There was some comfort in sharing these concerns with another sufferer. It was reassuring to learn of someone else's feeling of insecurity. An older member of the staff, wearing a sports jacket and sporting a rather flamboyant tie with a matching handkerchief in the breast pocket introduced himself to us. He had not spoken at the staff meeting. In fact he had been sitting quite near me and I had been somewhat surprised that he was preoccupied with the *Telegraph* crossword puzzle most of the time. However, he seemed friendly, bought us a drink and began to talk. His comments were seemingly casual; they might even have been rehearsed. Clearly he rejoiced in no fancy title in the hierarchy and struck a sympathetic chord by saying how bewildering it must seem to new arrivals like us. He offered us some gratuitous advice about how to survive the first days and months. He told us which Deputy Head to confide in and which to avoid, which department had the most money to spend, who to talk to in the staffroom if you wanted what you said to reach the Head, and the importance of getting on the right side of the 'trinity', the caretaker, the bursar and the Head's secretary. His remarks were amusing, sometimes slanderous, but I began to feel forearmed against imminent disaster. I realised that it would be wise to approach everyone with caution and make a particular effort to get on the right side of the non-teaching staff. There had been no mention of this in the staff handbook.

The set-up seemed more complicated than the factory where I had obtained some work experience. There the induction had been gradual and easily assimilated. The firm had a clear in-line management structure. At carefully appointed times I had visited various people who had guided me through the procedures. Everything had been supervised by a personnel officer. Each person I had visited explained how they fitted into the structure of the organisation. My immediate superior had taken a whole morning to show me the factory in operation. I had the opportunity to observe people at work. I was told precisely what I would be expected to do the next day. I was not left alone to do the job until I was familiar with it and had tried out the precise operations under supervision.

I returned to the school feeling slightly affected by the unaccustomed alcohol at lunchtime. In the afternoon there were faculty meetings with more talk of examination results, of the surprises and the disappointments. Nothing more could have been expected from that particular fifth year with the worst paper that had been set for years. Someone gave me a piece of paper which was apparently my timetable for the year, adding the comment. 'Sorry about the three periods of Geography, quite unavoidable this year, or so the timetablers say. I know it's not really your subject.' On this paper were symbols and numbers the meaning of which was not too clear. In the other hand I found myself clutching another piece of paper on which were the first-year arrangements for pupils. There were special arrangements for the new children, but there seemed to be no mention of new teachers and what they should do! There would be rooms to be found, assemblies to attend, books to be issued and, above all, children to be encountered in classrooms, in corridors, in the playground and possibly in bus queues. There seemed to be no special arrangements for new teachers, except that the Head had said something about her deputy having a responsibility for probationary teachers among her many duties. She had added that when the new term was under way there would be some weekly seminars. I wondered what they would be about. It all sounded a bit late in the day. What worried me was the following morning. What would happen with Form 4F? This was a class I had heard described as the problem form of that year. I wondered where their room was and whether they would be there. I also wondered what would happen if someone asked me a question and I didn't know the answer. When I eventually left the school to drive back to my flat there were still quite a number of unanswered queries.

2. January: developing strategies for coping

That first term seemed a lifetime, but eventually I got through it and survived Christmas in school, a hectic sequence of plays, parties and discos interspersed with hurriedly written reports. We frantically thought up questions for mock examination papers and more often lifted questions out of past examination papers. This was a particularly stressful time for new teachers and we were swept along by it all. There were deadlines for completing form lists and reports and somehow we managed to meet them. Then came the relief of a Christmas holiday.

When I returned to school in January some of the immediate anxieties had begun to disappear. I seemed to have orientated myself within the immediate circle of the faculty and of the children I was teaching. Short-term problems were replaced by longer-term anxieties. There was first and foremost the pressure of lessons to prepare and the persistent problems of individual children and difficult classes. These anxieties didn't go away and they were not easy to share with others. If I mentioned the names of certain children in the staffroom there were sometimes words of sympathy from colleagues, but more often a knowing look or a raised eyebrow. More confident colleagues exhibited mild surprise that I was having difficulty with that particular class. No one made it their business to come looking for my difficulties. They had enough of their own. I was reminded of my status as a probationary teacher by the fact that my head of faculty, one of the Deputies and, on one occasion, a visiting

L.E.A. adviser had each referred to 'the report' which apparently had to be written about me sometime. They had intimated that they would have to come into some of my classes. However, there was plenty of time for that when I had settled down. I think I would have appreciated some help earlier. The Deputy Head held some meetings of probationary teachers during lunch breaks, but other duties seemed to intervene and it was difficult to get all the young teachers together. Most of the meetings were interrupted by boys or girls knocking on the door or by the ringing of the telephone. Some of my problems I shared with other young teachers like myself. Together we found out which of the senior staff were helpful and sympathetic. Together we discovered which routines were important and needed to be followed and which could be ignored without fear of the consequences. Together we explored the folklore of the school, the unwritten rules which seemed to have evolved, but which kept the place running.

What dawned on me gradually was the extent to which I was on my own, in a classroom with children for most of my time. I had been given a timetable, some lists of children in forms and in sets and I had issued textbooks and exercise books to them. There was a syllabus and there were even schemes of work in some subject areas. Between these written documents and what happened in the classroom there seemed to be a great gap. There was certainly very little connection between the theory I had learnt and the practice of teaching. I began to realise that I lived a very solitary professional life as a teacher. I did not stand up in a courtroom with other lawyers present to demonstrate my skill in pleading a case and I did not join a team of experienced doctors in an operating theatre. The opportunity to see other teachers teaching happened very rarely indeed.

Whatever guidelines there were, I was left to interpret them myself. On duty at break, during lunchtime or with a bus queue I handled quite large groups of children, usually recalling how it was done when I was at school. I devised certain strategies for coping. I learned how to organise my time for preparation and for marking children's work. I came to know which classes needed careful preparation and which books needed marking next. I began to acquire a rudimentary survival kit for the classroom. I got to know which classes I had to be firm with, which classes I could have a joke with and which individual children I should never lose sight of even when my back was apparently turned.

I was left very much to manage my own affairs. My head of faculty did give me some help but when I wanted him he was usually teaching. There were faculty meetings when I could raise problems but they seemed very unimportant compared with the topics we usually discussed. These meetings were usually held after school when everybody who had taught all day was anxious to get away. Once textbooks and syllabuses had been issued I was on my own. There were lots of other things to prepare: worksheets to design, maps to duplicate, lesson notes to work out. I had prepared lessons before during teaching practice but now I was teaching for twenty hours every week. Once I got into a classroom there was no more time for preparation. Teaching is a very pragmatic activity and I solved most of my problems as they came along. I answered questions, I dealt with interruptions and I thought on my feet. There were good days. On a good day life was exhilarating. The many encounters with children were stimulating. On a bad day there were conflicts and rows. Stress took its toll and sometimes I couldn't sleep or suffered from headaches at weekends. So much depended on other people and the most important people in my life were children. I spent far more of my time with them than with adults.

There were areas of school life, however, of which I knew little or nothing. There were teachers who did less teaching than others, but I had little idea of how they spent their spare time. It was certainly not clear to me why some teachers were paid higher salaries than others. They had titles, but what they did to justify these titles was not at all clear. Some had nicknames which were used in the staffroom, such as the 'managing director' and 'the shop steward'. Many had nicknames used by the children. I often wondered where to go when a problem arose – to a form tutor, to a head of faculty, to a head of year – and sometimes I wondered whether there was someone else whose title I had forgotten. I gathered that the Head had a big diagram in her room in the shape of a pyramid. It listed all our names and I must have been right at the bottom. She also had little photographs of each of us next to our names. Perhaps she couldn't always remember what we all did either.

3. June: taking on further responsibilities

I suppose it was my own fault that I became involved in so many things. I should have kept my mouth shut as I had enough to do preparing lessons and keeping abreast of the marking. It was all I could do to squeeze in some social life at the weekends.

It all began on sports day when we were hanging about waiting for the rain to stop. I fell into conversation with my head of faculty, Martin Wragg, and he raised the question of worksheets for the second-year courses. I recalled that at the last faculty meeting I had voiced, hesitatingly, my concern about the existing worksheets, wondering if they could be improved. Martin now asked me if I would be prepared to have a go at a workscheme for the second year for all our colleagues to use. I was taken aback at first. It had not been in my mind when I had originally suggested the idea and I doubted whether I had the expertise or authority to tackle it. However, I suppose I was flattered to be asked and I agreed. The Deputy Head (Pastoral) had already seen me about looking after a form the following September and the head of Drama had extracted from me a promise to give a hand with the next production. There was also a possibility of taking charge of one of the junior school teams. I had also sought permission of the Head to attend a course for six afternoons in the autumn term. Perhaps that was a bit rash. I was also going to take on some examination classes in September. All these invitations served to boost my morale and had led me to feel more confident, but suddenly I had some qualms as to whether I was taking on too much.

Later that same afternoon after helping out with the high jump I was chatting to an older colleague and happened to tell him of the request to prepare a scheme of work for the second year. He expressed sympathy rather than congratulations and harped more on the extra work involved than on the compliment which I thought was being paid to me. He added ruefully that in the old days such a request would have been accompanied by the award of an extra allowance and a title to go with it. This tangible recognition of my first steps on the ladder of promotion was now, it seemed, a forlorn hope.

Several weeks later the Head sent for me and I found myself going into her room for the first time since my appointment although I had met her occasionally about the school. She asked whether I had enjoyed my first year's teaching and I gave a suitably enthusiastic response. There was certainly no time to recount all that had happened. She enquired about my future hopes and I talked about the various invitations I had received to take on more responsibility. There seemed to be a tacit assumption that progress professionally meant taking on more things, particularly things which happened outside the classroom. Relationships with children and greater effectiveness as a teacher in the classroom were important, but increasing my experience seemed more a matter of becoming involved in other sorts of activities. So when the Head closed the conversation by asking me to take over the Duke of Edinburgh Award Scheme in the lower school (or to provide some help with the library or to give some assistance with examination arrangements) and with no extra money, I agreed, of course.

Upon reflection, I began to wonder exactly what was a teacher's main job. Was it teaching or was it all these other activities? Would I be able to find time for these other undertakings as well as prepare lessons and mark books? If there wasn't enough time to do both, then which would suffer?

Questions for discussion

1. How do the experiences of this young teacher compare with your own?
2. To what extent did the experience of initial training prepare you for your first experiences as a teacher? Which of your early experiences as a teacher did you feel least prepared for?
3. Do you consider that it is the job of initial training to prepare young teachers for the practical business of teaching or does it have other more important objectives?
4. What can a school do to receive young teachers and prepare them for their early experiences of teaching?
5. Does an L.E.A. and its advisory service have any responsibilities for providing support for young teachers? Discuss the value of in-service training for those in their first year of teaching. What forms of such training have you found to be effective?
6. Describe the 'strategies for coping' which you acquired when you began to teach. Can these be learned beforehand, in the course of in-service training or do they have to be learned on the job?
7. 'The only way to improve the teaching skills of a young teacher is for him or her to receive feedback on performance from an experienced practitioner.' Discuss the advantages and the problems of providing this form of staff development in a school.
8. Do you consider that a formal system of staff performance appraisal would help to maintain and improve the quality of teaching among young teachers? What form might it take?
9. Does reducing the teaching load of the new entrant ease induction difficulties, or prolong the distinction between a learner and a trained teacher?
10. Does seeing the new entrant as a manager, albeit a junior or trainee one, help or hinder the commencement of one's career as a teacher?

In-service project work

1. Design an induction programme for young teachers at your school. Suggest what individuals can do to help them through their first year's teaching.
2. Keep a diary of your professional activities as a teacher during one week (including the weekend). Make a note of the approximate

time spent on various tasks such as teaching classes, marking children's work, preparing lessons, attending meetings, meeting parents, preparing teaching materials or any other activities. What proportion of your time was spent on each of these jobs?
3. Arrange to have one of your lessons observed by a colleague and then ask for some feedback on your performance and that of the class.

Chapter 4

Managing for Learning

The first experiences of a young teacher: all teachers are managers

A young teacher on the first morning of the first day in his or her first job may appear to be a strange point of departure from which to explore management in schools. We believe that this is precisely where school management does begin.

When the young teacher arrives in the staffroom of his first school he has completed his initial training. His qualifications as a teacher have provided him with entry into a profession. He has practised teaching real children during his training period. If he is typical of student teachers he will have found that teaching practice was the most valuable part of his training because it represented a real situation for however brief a period. He was no longer talking about teaching or listening to others talk about teaching, he was doing it.

Nevertheless, the first experiences of our young teacher on taking up his appointment in a school are daunting. The initial unfamiliarity with the plant and the personnel is confusing. The volume of work is formidable. The encounters with large numbers of children are an ordeal. There are children in forms and in sets. There are children in large informal groups in corridors, in playgrounds and in assembly halls. They all have different names and different moods. Some are interested and enthusiastic. Others are indifferent or aggressive. In any one group there is a sea of faces, eyeing him with curiosity and weighing up their new teacher. He is acutely aware of his newness.

The sheer number of lessons to prepare contrasts sharply with the slower pace and careful preparation which was possible during his periods of teaching practice. Instead of a leisurely sequence of lesson notes prepared and lessons given there is now a desperate struggle to survive. Our young teacher describes on p.23 how he is 'swept along' and what a stressful experience the end of term is for all young teachers. Time is at a premium as he strives to retain the initiative which will be wrested from him by some children if he faces them inadequately prepared in teaching materials or in teaching skills.

The school to which he has come to exercise his professional skills seems somewhat reluctant to interfere in the area of relationships between teacher and child. The teacher in our case study receives very little help in these early days and even on his first day there are no special arrangements for new teachers (p.22). There appears to be an unwritten law that this relationship between teacher and taught is sacrosanct. It is almost a sign of weakness to discuss difficult children informally (p.23). Like other professions, teaching has its folklore and once you begin to examine the business of teaching and learning you enter a realm of myths, mystique and, perhaps, even magic. If you ask questions such as 'what makes a good teacher?', you enter a protracted professional debate without any certainty of emerging with a clear answer. It is not the purpose of this book to enter that debate, but lest we should be criticised for advocating that a few managerial 'tricks of the trade' will make a 'good teacher', we want to recognise at the outset that there is a quality of magic which invests good teaching with a uniqueness and which often defies description or analysis. The skills, and indeed the art, which a skilled teacher employs in a classroom are idiosyncratic, personal and often unpredictable. However, having acknowledged that there is an element of mystery which surrounds successful teaching and learning, it is our purpose to make the case that successful teachers employ a range of skills and strategies which are essentially practical in nature and which greatly increase the effectiveness of their teaching. These skills and strategies we term managerial. Some are of a routine nature and are intended to form habits in the behaviour of learners, others are of an emergency nature designed to ward off chaos and calamity. The happenings in a classroom are not unlike those in a theatre, with both teachers and taught taking part in the drama. While the quality of the total experience depends ultimately on the integrity of the performance and the event has its own magic, nevertheless the effectiveness of the whole will be greatly improved by competent stage management. Sometimes it may even depend on being able to carry on when the scenery collapses. It is at this level of practicality that the key to success or failure of many a lesson lies. The expertise and competence of our young teacher in the case study would have been greatly strengthened in the early days if he had been equipped with the managerial skills for coping to which we refer. As it was he acquired many of them on the job, learning what he calls the 'unwritten rules', and the 'strategies for coping' which make up 'the survival kit' (p.24). He worked out his own set of priorities for preparing lessons, marking children's work and maintaining discipline (p.24).

Management and the teacher

The definition of management which we adopt is getting things done by, through or with other people. A class teacher exercises management skills when getting children to do things which may lead to learning. He or she gets children to solve problems, perform experiments, read books, discuss and carry out a whole range of activities which enable learning to take place. This, however, is not management as generally considered in a school. The word in that context is used to describe those activities in which adults get other adults to do things. There is no reason for this limited use of the term 'management'. A good teacher is concerned that children should do certain things. The fact that children do or do not do these things is evidence of whether learning has or has not taken place. What is more, a teacher has a very broad degree of autonomy in this activity of organising and managing his teaching. The young teacher in the previous case study discovered that he had a frightening degree of freedom and he confesses to feeling very much alone with his classes (p.24). The induction scheme for new teachers seems to have been very half-hearted and the proposed meetings for new teachers were not taken very seriously (p.24). Yet teaching was the major job for which he was being employed.

In our view this direct responsibility for children's learning is the main feature of a teacher's professional life and is the most important activity which happens in a school.

At present, management is commonly separated from the activity of teaching and is seen as comprising all the other jobs which have to be done, such as running a faculty, organising examinations, arranging and administering option schemes and timetabling. The managers are Heads, Deputy Heads, faculty heads or heads of subject departments. We seek to give greater priority to children's learning as the central feature of the teacher's professionalism and we see the management of learning as the major managerial task of a school, to which all the other managerial tasks mentioned above should contribute. All teachers manage learning.

Levels of management in schools: junior, middle and senior

This major managerial task begins in classrooms, in laboratories, in workshops, on visits to foreign countries or during outdoor activities on mountainsides. It happens wherever teachers seek to maximise the effectiveness of learning. Those managerial activities associated closely with learning situations we term 'junior management' and the role of junior managers is carried out by any teacher when teaching children, no matter what other title this teacher may hold. He or she may be a Head, a head of faculty or a class teacher with no other responsibilities.

Tasks of management are, of course, carried out at other levels in a school. There are many teams of teachers working in schools, as members of faculties or of subject departments, or as pastoral tutors of year groups. Such a faculty team may meet to thrash out the objectives of a certain piece of teaching material and may attempt to reach a consensus as to how these objectives should be turned into classroom activity. This team is carrying out a task which we term 'middle management'. Again, the team may include a Deputy Head, a careers teacher or a head of year as well as a number of class teachers. The head of faculty may chair such a group.

Likewise, groups of teachers meet to discuss and decide on matters which affect the whole school. Such a group may discuss a change in the balance of the curriculum in the fourth and fifth years of a secondary school, and may take a decision to reduce the number of optional subjects being offered. This group is carrying out a task which we describe as 'senior management' and again it may include a Head, a Deputy Head responsible for the curriculum, heads of subject departments and also class teachers. The inclusion of class teachers in the latter group may cause surprise and requires some explanation.

Teachers in multiple roles: some implications for school organisation

It is evident from the preceding section that teachers perform multiple roles and this is an important factor which distinguishes schools from other organisations. A teacher of history may also be a year tutor and be involved in either of the decision-making groups described above. He or she may also be in charge of a football or netball team, take skiing parties abroad and play second violin in the school orchestra. In other words, it is possible for a teacher to perform junior, middle and senior management tasks; in fact, it is quite normal for a teacher to do so. We believe that this performance of multiple roles by teachers has important implications for the organisation of schools.

For a long period of their development secondary schools were organised as autocracies. In a paper published in 1956, Baron traced the development in the mid-nineteenth century of the distinctive 'headmaster tradition' in the English public schools and showed how the tradition was later emulated with minor modifications in the new maintained secondary schools of the early twentieth century. A powerful and distinctive role concept emerged of the Head as a benevolent autocrat. Baron noted few signs of significant change at the time of writing. Changes in secondary school organisation began to take place in the 1970s as schools grew in size. Writing elsewhere, Buckley states:

> The growth of large comprehensive schools led to more elaborate hierarchical structures, which meant a differentiation of the head's functions. The secondary schools thus became more bureaucratic and there was a concern for delegation and for establishing structures for decision-making. (Buckley, 1985).

However, hierarchial structures did not really suit schools because they did not have an in-line style of management. Teachers continued to perform multiple roles and decision making took place in various groups, teams, committees and working parties which functioned in what may be described as a collegiate or 'loosely coupled system'. The steep hierarchy did not recognise that all teachers, whatever other responsibilities they have, are primarily responsible for the quality of teaching and learning. Nor did it recognise that they all perform junior, middle and senior managerial tasks. While a hierarchy is necessary for administrative purposes in the posts of Heads, Deputy Heads and heads of faculties or subject departments, we believe that the organisation should be 'shallower' and the present hierarchies reduced. Above all, the appropriate organisation of a secondary school should recognise the responsibility of all teachers for teaching and learning, and allow all the opportunity to participate in the major policy decisions.

The participative mode of management: the forum

The groups of teachers described above perform managerial tasks at junior, middle and senior levels. Any teacher may operate at any of these levels. We seek to extend this system by reshaping the decision-making structure for all major policy making at the senior level. Instead of such decisions being taken by a small senior management team surrounding the Head, we advocate a decision-making body which formalises the opportunity for all teachers to share in all major policy decisions. This is the forum which all teachers in a secondary school may attend if they so wish. We shall describe its form more fully and illustrate its function in a case study later (p.131).

However, while we believe that all members of a teaching staff have a right to participate in major policy-making as members of the forum, it must be stressed that there remains a clear role for a senior management team. Their task is to implement the decisions taken at the formal meetings of the forum. They are the executive and not the sole legislature. They share in the decision making with their colleagues. They also have the responsibility for seeing that these decisions are carried out.

An approach to managing secondary schools: unified, appropriate and participative

The approach to managing schools which this book advocates may be summed up as unified, appropriate and participative. It is a unified approach in that it recognises that all teachers, and not just some, are managers. One aspect of the professionalism of all teachers is to manage at junior, middle or senior level. It is appropriate because it recognises that certain features of school organisation are quite specific to schools and therefore require the application of management principles which are suitable for them. It is, above all, the learning process which is being managed. It is participative in that all the teachers in a school have a corporate professional responsibility for the quality of the teaching and learning which goes on in a school. It follows that they should participate in the major decisions affecting the life of the school.

The need for such a unified, appropriate and participative management in secondary schools will be more essential as opportunities for promotion become fewer. New entrants to the profession will spend a much longer time teaching in classrooms and on a main professional grade of salary. Teaching will remain the major activity of most teachers for most of their professional lives. Class teachers, heads of subject departments, those in pastoral posts, Deputies and Heads, in fact all teachers, will look for a management system which gives them a stake in their schools and the possibility of personal and professional development within it.

If teachers are all involved in the running of their schools and if there is recognition not only in attitudes but in financial rewards that teaching children is their major task, then there will be greater cohesion in the profession and a greater commitment in the schools.

Suggestions for further reading

D.E.S. (1977) *Ten Good Schools: A secondary school enquiry* (London, H.M.S.O.)

D.E.S. (1979) *Aspects of Secondary Education in England* (London, H.M.S.O.)

HANDY, C. and AITKEN, R. (1986) *Understanding Schools as Organisations* (London, Penguin).

HANDY, C.B. (1985) *Taken for granted. Understanding schools as organisations* (London, Longmans).

RUTTER, M. *et al.* (1979) *Fifteen Thousand Hours* (London, Open Books).

References

BARON. G. (1956), 'Some aspects of the "Headmaster Tradition"' in *Researches and Studies 14, 1-16* (Reprinted in: Musgrove, P. W. (Ed) *Sociology, History and Education*, London, Methuen).

BUCKLEY, J.P. (1985) *The training of secondary school heads in Western Europe* (Windsor, N.F.E.R.-NELSON).

Chapter 5

Case Studies: Junior Management

1. Preparation: the gap between the syllabus and the lesson

It was Sunday evening and as usual I had only just got round to thinking about the next week's lessons and in particular to wondering about Form 3L. I knew where I had got to the previous week and I had last year's lesson notes. In fact, those notes went back several years. Now we had the new syllabus, but that didn't seem to help very much. The syllabus had been reviewed recently as part of a curriculum study throughout the school. A number of faculty meetings had been held after school to review the aims of the subject and to reappraise the content. We had even got down to an analysis of the concepts, skills and attitudes which we were teaching through the subject. This process of enquiry was time consuming, but was intellectually stimulating. The members of the faculty had all participated and even Jim Thorpe, a senior colleague who was taking early retirement at the end of the summer term, thought it was worthwhile. He said it was the first time he had engaged in that sort of discussion with his colleagues in the whole of his career. Our head of faculty was very enthusiastic about it all and claimed that it would now be much easier to see where the subject fitted into the school's whole curriculum. The new syllabus was supposed to clarify everyone's thinking and make the preparation of lessons more straightforward. But did it in fact do this?

The aims of the subject were set down clearly and so was the intention to test and assess whether any learning had happened. Between these two statements of intent there seemed to be a great gap; namely, a lack of any explanation of what actually happened in the classroom. My immediate problem was what was going to happen in my classroom with that class, 3L, that week. We had all spent a great deal of time examining what was to be taught but very little time asking how it was to be taught. The way we taught the subject seemed to be left to each one of us.

A number of questions occurred to me as I thought about 3L. What was I going to do and what were the children going to do? These were questions of action. What materials was I going to provide? How many or how much? What activities were the children going to engage in? Would they be talking, discussing or writing? What was I going to tell them and what would they discover for themselves? Would I be able to keep them occupied and would I set them any homework?

I was well aware that these questions should have been tackled long ago. In fact they were questions which kept coming up when I was planning lessons. It wasn't that I didn't prepare lessons. I had come back to school in September with a great deal of prepared material, but once the term had begun to gather momentum everything started piling up. Time, or the lack of it, is a major problem which faces each teacher. There never seemed to be enough time to prepare adequately for all the lessons which filled my timetable during a week. When I had first started teaching I had been quite overwhelmed by the amount of preparation and marking. These two activities had vied with each other for priority as I had struggled to keep my head above water. Things had gradually improved as I gained experience, by learning on the job, but the problem remained as I thought about each new week's lessons. What were the activities which would enable learning to take place? Was I going to talk about the topic or demonstrate it? If it was to be illustrated then by what means? Would the children just listen passively or were they going to talk about it, discuss it, draw it, experiment, solve problems or what? At the end of the lesson what would they have acquired, new knowledge or a new skill? How would I know whether they had learned anything?

It would have been helpful if the members of the faculty had discussed this sort of thing, the methodology of the subject, what was actually going to happen. Or perhaps it would have been helpful if we had discussed our experience of teaching certain 'key' lessons when particularly important topics were being taught. It might have been even more helpful if we had observed each other teach some of these lessons and then discussed them afterwards, together. Such key lessons might have served as 'markers' to chart a way through the syllabus. Such a framework of key lessons worked out jointly by members of the faculty would certainly have been a great help to everyone.

To a number of my colleagues all this did not seem a problem. Their lesson notes had served them well. Some were tattered and timeless. These notes were written up on a blackboard and were copied into exercise books by children as a ritual routine. They were then learned off by heart and the material regurgitated at the next examination. It was all disarmingly simple and relatively little preparation was necessary. There were times when I too had resorted to this strategy, but I was under no illusion that concepts or skills were acquired in that way. If the aim was to teach these, then other methods were necessary, which took much more time and care to prepare. If there was to be activity on the part of the children, instead of passivity, if they were to be doing things instead of just sitting and listening, if they were to be discussing, experimenting, making, observing or constructing, then the form of the lesson was far more complex to prepare and the new syllabus did not describe how to do that.

So, I asked myself, what were 3L going to do and what was I going to do to prepare for them to do it?

2. Lesson: what was planned and what happened

I was sitting in the staffroom after break and experiencing a vague sense of unease and dissatisfaction which I sometimes felt after a lesson. I had been looking forward to taking Form 3L because they were a cheerful, lively lot who seemed to enjoy the subject and on the whole worked well. I had prepared the lesson with some care, following a pattern which I often used. I was going to start with some oral questions on past work, then give the lesson proper, introducing the new work and finally set some practical class work based on it. I had prepared a printed sheet of notes and a worksheet to go with it. It had all looked fine. I was reasonably organised and felt in good form as I entered the classroom.

However, things did not go too well from the start. When I entered the room I did not see the funny side of a drawing on the blackboard. I wasn't quite sure whether it was intended to be me, but it was certainly crude. I had it rubbed off quickly by a boy and expressed my annoyance by one or two terse comments about amateur cartoonists in the class. The class had gone silent and then there was a snigger from the back. The response to my first few oral questions was slow and muted. I had to work hard to get them going and even then there seemed to be some private joke going on which I found irritating. I decided to cut short the questions, without being sure that the previous work had been fully understood, but time was pressing. I had a key lesson prepared and was anxious to get on with it as soon as

possible to ensure that I got through all the practical work before the
bell rang. I gave out the papers which I had duplicated, but even this
simple operation did not pass off without incident. The pack of
papers which I asked a reliable child to distribute went around her
half of the class quickly enough, but the boy given the other batch of
papers dropped half of them and there was noise and some confusion
while these were being retrieved from under various desks. By now
five minutes had passed and I was anxious to be teaching what I had
planned to teach, without any more interruption.

While I was going through the new work on the blackboard the class
was fairly attentive, although some were perhaps quiet because they
were busy reading the duplicated sheets which I had given out.
Certainly my occasional questions concerning the blackboard
examples seemed to find some members of the class rather distracted.
This meant going over some of the work again for the sake of those
who had not understood what I was trying to demonstrate the first
time. I was reasonably patient although becoming anxious that there
would be insufficient time for the practical work which had to be done
before the end of the lesson. It was essential that the class had the
experience of handling the ideas themselves if they were really going
to grasp them.

Some children had set to work on these examples without delay, but
others did not seem at all clear as to what they had to do. It took more
time to deal with these questions and when everyone in the class was
settled and working there did not seem to be much of the lesson
remaining. I had hoped to collect in the worksheets in order to mark
them before I next saw the class but there was clearly no chance of
everyone finishing on time. They would have to finish off the
exercises for homework. That was not very satisfactory but there was
nothing else for it. When I announced this to the class, there was a
chorus of dissent; not an outcry, more a rumble of discontent. Some
pupils stopped work and began to pack their belongings into their
bags. I reminded them that the bell hadn't yet gone. They smiled and
slowly took out an odd pen or a book without enthusiasm.

The bell rang while all this was happening and immediately
everybody began packing their belongings, standing up and jostling
to leave the room. I repeated my instructions about the homework
over the noise as they hurried out. Apparently it was P.E. next and
they had to get over to the sports hall and get changed.

I slowly gathered up my own books and papers and left the empty
room. No, it had not been one of my most successful or most satisfying

lessons. Why? Was it the timing or the class or just me? I suppose it was all of these factors. Once a lesson starts anything may happen, however well it has been planned, prepared and timed. There is bound to be an unpredictable element where children and relationships are concerned. It would have been much worse if I had not prepared it at all. At least I managed to get through the key lesson and a good deal of the practical work had been done. Perhaps it wasn't such a bad lesson after all.

3. Lessons and teachers: what the children said

Students in their third year of secondary education and attending two different schools were asked what they considered made a good or a bad lesson and what made for a good or a bad teacher. The following quotations are some of their replies.

'A poor lesson is when the work has nothing to do with life when you leave school; a lot of the Maths we do we will never use again.'

'A good teacher has a sense of humour . . . is helpful with your work, and understands how hard some work is. Miss A . . . is always pleasant and always helps you when you get stuck.'

'My ideal lesson is one where the work is varied when you can draw as well as write. I think that all teachers should vary their work. A bad lesson is when we have to copy from a sheet. Last week we had to write out a Biology worksheet for a double lesson, but the R.E. lessons usually let us draw pictures, write a bit and discuss.'

'I think a bad teacher is someone who rambles on, in the same tone of voice, all lesson. I dislike a teacher who is moody. We have Mr B . . . who has a dreamy voice. Mr C . . . who takes us for P.E. is all right some days, but last Wednesday he was angry when he came into the changing room, and shouted at us all lesson.'

'A bad lesson is one where you have to sit and write in silence. You dare not speak in Mr F's lessons.'

'I think that a bad teacher is one who cannot control the class, shouts at everybody for no reason, looks scruffy and treats pupils as animals.'

'I enjoy a lesson like Personal and Social education, when we can discuss things, act out situations and watch films and slides.'

'I think teachers should be able to take a joke, not bite your head off when you do not understand. It is not fair when you cannot voice your own opinions.'

'We have a teacher who is forever stopping and starting the lesson, and that does not help you learn.'

'I think Mrs C . . . is a good teacher; she is kind but strict, shouts when you are naughty, but is mostly nice and cheerful every time you see her.'

'Mrs H . . . cannot take a joke, and never seems to listen to me.'

'I have the opinion that Mr J . . . is a bad teacher, because he cannot control the class, threatens pupils with detentions, does not mark books and talks on when no one is listening.'

'My worst lessons are when I am stuck and the teacher will not help me.'

'Mr K . . . does not explain anything, makes you sit boy next to girl, and sounds like a sergeant major in the army.'

'I enjoy Home Economics, because you know what you have to do, and it's full of different things. Mathematics is one lesson where you do the same thing for the whole time.'

'Mr L . . . lets you have a class discussion, and then sets an interesting task which would involve things like a bit of writing, a bit of drawing and a bit of group work.'

'Mr A . . . is a good teacher because he is strict with those who do wrong, and does not take it out on the whole class.'

'I think that the best lessons are those when you decide what work you want to do like a project in Design, and then work on it on your own.'

'I like Mr P . . . because he does not have pets and treats everyone the same.'

'Some of my teachers talk all the time and seem to think that they are better than you.'

'The lessons I like best are those like Geography where you do educational games; they help you to remember things.'

'The best teacher I have is Mr R . . . because he has a great sense of humour.'

'I think that a good teacher should be kind, understanding and fair, and if they have had a bad morning they should not take their problems out on the students. Our head of year never does this, but some teachers do this all the time.'

'A good teacher should be a person who is cheerful, understanding, helpful and a good listener. We have Miss D . . . for French and we work better for her because she asks us what we think and listens to our ideas.'

'Mrs E . . . is frequently in a bad mood, gets you to copy books when she does not feel like teaching you, and does not like you asking for help.'

'Our History lessons are boring because we have to write all the time, and the teacher does not talk about what you are doing.'

'The type of lesson I like is like our Geography lessons, when all the class is involved, and there is not the same people answering questions all the time. I do not mind working hard so long as the work is interesting.'

'A bad lesson is when you have to copy from the blackboard. Some days we do a lot of that.'

'A good teacher is someone who cares and who gives the right punishment to people who deserve it . . . someone who you can trust with your problems.'

'Mrs S . . . is a teacher who seems to like children and can get on with them. She always looks at both sides of a story: she listens and is fair.'

'Our form tutor is a good teacher. He treats you like a human being and not as if you are a half-wit, even if you are!'

'For me, a good lesson has to have a good atmosphere to work in. Not all of it should be writing, but some of it should be talking and discussing things. The teachers I like best all let us talk.'

4. Resources: some problems with technical aids

It is the end of the mid morning break. You finish your cup of coffee
and the staffroom begins to empty as teachers go off to their classes.
As you grab an armful of exercise books and a sheaf of papers you
suddenly remember you need a box of slides for this lesson. Who
borrowed them for a parallel class? You think it was Gail: fortunately
she's very reliable and will have put them back in the cupboard in your
room. You rush down the corridor and up the stairs to find the class
already in the room and settling down. Your routine of always having
someone to give out the books seems to be working. In like manner
the exercise books are quickly removed from your desk and
distributed. The class is instructed to do their corrections while you
look for the slide projector and the slides. The projector is soon found,
but what about the extension lead? It doesn't seem to be in its
customary place. A boy is despatched next door to a colleague who will
doubtless be able to help, but the message comes back that a number
of such leads have been borrowed by the Drama department for the
play which is being put on next week. The same boy volunteers to go
in pursuit of the elusive lead. You fill in time by a slightly longer
introduction to the subject of the lesson and by the time your minion
returns you are all ready with the slide magazine at the ready and
loaded onto the projector. Everything is switched on and works, with
only one slight snag: the first slide is upside down. Sniggers from the
class are quickly subdued by passing on to others in a rapid sequence.
That is to say, a fairly rapid sequence because the slides are not exactly
sequential, and in some cases distinctly inconsequential. This is
becoming a trifle annoying and is causing mild amusement to the
class, particularly when it is necessary to read some of the words
backwards. Somebody has been at these slides you suspect, and your
suspicions are directed at Gail. Anyhow, the class take it all in very
good part and soon the sequence comes to an end. In fact it is brought
to a slightly premature conclusion by what must be a loose connection.
This produces a blinking effect as the slide appears and disappears
somewhat intermittently. You decide to call it a day and get down to
the class work.

Again, your minion rapidly distributes the worksheets and you are
starting to give instructions when two pupils at the back put their
hands up. They are short of worksheets. You assure them that they
can't be because you brought in just the right number. They
apologetically hold up two sheets of plain paper which the duplicator

has perversely ignored. Things are not going quite as you had hoped but a willing volunteer dispatched to the staff room quickly returns with another batch of papers marked '4F 34 copies'. Two are extracted from this pack and all is well. Well, nearly all. Your instructions are crystal clear and there are no questions. The class has heads down and everyone is beavering away. What is not so clear is the quality of the duplicating which seems to fade inexplicably at certain places on each sheet producing a blurred effect and some interesting suggestions as to what the missing information might be from members of the class. This problem, is however, readily solved by writing the whole of the indeterminate paragraph on the blackboard. You have always prided yourself on your blackboard presentation anyway and have not gone in for those fancy overhead projector things. The bulbs are always going in them.

The class is commendably hard at work when the bell goes and it seems a pity that most have only got halfway down the first side of the worksheet when it's time to pack up. Your over-zealous minion has, in fact, collected in a large number when you decide to have them given out again and finished off for homework. By now people are disgorging through the door to a Science lesson. You hope they got the instructions for the homework. They were very clear and you shouted them quite loud enough.

As you put away your equipment you make a mental note to get those slides sorted out before you need them next. You must also have words with the reprographics people about the quality of the duplicating. On second thoughts perhaps it would be better to bring it up at a departmental meeting. Those secretaries easily take offence.

Back in the staffroom you sink into a chair and light a cigarette. When you speak to the head of department about the duplicating, perhaps it wouldn't be a bad idea to ask what the chances are of an in-service course in the school for newcomers on such things as projectors and reprographics; in fact, on the whole business of producing teaching materials? You might then even be able to risk using the overhead projector or perhaps some of those splendid video-recordings. A short three-day course for new arrivals shouldn't be too difficult to arrange. The chap from the Science department who pinched your extension leads is a wizard with all that technology. He's just the man to run such a course and he might be rather glad to be asked. He hasn't a special allowance for anything and it would give him a bit of kudos as well as help you and other colleagues to come to terms with all these modern gadgets. Your reverie is interrupted by the bell and by Gail asking to borrow a blackboard rubber.

5. Managing the environment: enlivening the atmosphere from unpromising beginnings

You were delighted to be promoted to number two in a department at a neighbouring school to that where you began your teaching career. The initial excitement of your new appointment is tinged with some anxiety when you take up the job and see the school at closer quarters. The atmosphere is very different from that at your previous school. That school had been built in the 1930s as a grammar school and was solid and unexciting. Nevertheless, on entering the building you were conscious of a lively and stimulating environment. The walls of corridors were covered with colourful examples of children's work which was changed frequently. Display cabinets were full of craft work in pottery and metal. Noticeboards were kept up-to-date and not left to harbour dog-eared dusty pieces of paper. This atmosphere had overflowed into classrooms and workshops where there were many displays of children's work. You had been swept along in this ethos of providing a stimulating and workmanlike environment for learning. You had inherited a room in which bare walls were covered with display board. There was plenty of storage, both cupboards and shelving. You had an overhead projector and screen. You had added to all this your own unsophisticated, but effective, retrieval system for worksheets. Everything was to hand and you did not have to go borrowing from colleagues when you needed a cassette player or a slide projector.

By comparison, your present school is very different. The building itself is much more promising, having been built in the late 1960s. It is light and airy. Walls are colour-washed or papered, windows have curtains. The differences lie in the atmosphere of the school. Everything has a neglected and tired look about it. There are displays of art work in some corridors but they have not been changed since last September and have gathered dust or been scribbled on. On close inspection, noticeboards reveal notices from last year, the paper grey by now. Your own room has a very depressing appearance. The first impression is of bare walls, desks in rows and one cupboard. Your head of department has explained that all equipment is held in a central departmental store in the interests of security. This also applies to books. There is little use of worksheets and only one overhead projector in the department. All this is very depressing and you are exercised as to how to remedy it. One answer is to accept the new ethos and adapt yourself to it in the belief that there is very little

you can do to change what is clearly the ethos of the school.
Everything in your previous experience reacts against that point of
view and the first few days of teaching in your new school confirm this
reaction. The experience of not having all your teaching materials to
hand delays or interrupts your teaching and disrupts the children's
learning. You soon become very irritated at having to draw equipment
from a central store and then return it at the end of the day.
Limitation on the number of exercise books and the amount of
stationery that you are allowed to carry in your own store cupboard is
a further source of annoyance. What are you to do?

You talk to your head of department, but he is anxious above all
about security. There have been a number of break-ins at the school.
There have also been cuts in departmental allowances and he wishes
to keep a close check on everything. You talk to junior colleagues and,
while some are sympathetic to your views, they are reluctant to
challenge the head of department's views. You, yourself, a recent
appointment, do not want to demonstrate apparent disloyalty so early
by raising the matter at a departmental meeting. Yet something must
be done because you are convinced that the children's learning
environment and your effectiveness as a teacher is dependent on both
the appearance of the classroom and the workshop atmosphere,
where equipment, books and stationery are all to hand. After all, your
colleagues teaching Science, Art, Crafts or Home Economics have
always adopted this principle without being questioned.

As you think through the problem various strategies come to mind.
You can seek a confrontation with the head of department, having
lobbied support for your point of view from your colleagues.
Alternatively, you can begin in a smaller way in your own room. The
layout of furniture can be altered and children's work can be
displayed. There is little display space and the wrath of the caretaker
may have to be risked if work is to be stuck to the wallpaper. You can
supplement these displays with fixtures and posters which illustrate
lessons in progress. You can introduce your rather ramshackle
retrieval system for workcards or worksheets. These measures are all
right as far as they go, but sooner or later the real problems of creating
a satisfactory working environment will have to be faced and this must
involve tackling the head of department about distributing the
equipment held centrally among the members of the department and
allowing each member to be much more autonomous and
independent.

One afternoon you are tidying up at the end of an afternoon,

having returned the slide projector and screen to the departmental
store. Your wife enters your room and looks around. She is a primary
school teacher and has come to pick you up in the car on the way
home. She looks at you thoughtfully and says, 'It's a bit different from
your last room isn't it? I wonder whether the children notice the
difference when they come up from the primary school? What are
you going to do about it?' 'I don't know', you reply, 'what difference do
you notice?'

'Well, it's the feel of it. It's the lack of colour, makes it feel cold and
drab. We are always told that we have to arouse curiosity and enquiry,
ask lots of questions. Perhaps that's just primary school stuff.' There is
a pause and it's your turn to look thoughtful.

'Yes, you're right. It has to give a message to the children doesn't it?
This is a place of work and what happens here matters. This room
doesn't do that – yet.'

6. Managing learning experiences: creating a variety of opportunities for learning

You have settled down in your new school as number two in the
department and have sorted out some of your immediate problems in
creating a room which is lively and stimulating for the children and in
which you have at least some of your teaching materials and
equipment readily available. In other words you have gone some way
towards producing the workshop atmosphere which is conducive to
effective teaching and learning. There have been some jibes from
older colleagues and your head of department has not taken much
notice. However, some younger colleagues have begun to seek you
out to talk about their concerns as to the way the department is being
run. Your head of department is 51 and has been teaching in the
school for twenty years, since the school opened. He was promoted to
his present post fifteen years ago and is now disappointed at lack of
promotion to Deputy Headship. He achieves consistently good
examination results with the top set at G.C.S.E. level and with the
small groups who take your subject at 'A' level.

The younger members of your department find opportunities to
voice a number of anxieties. According to them the courses offered
are very examination orientated, and little is specially prepared for
the less able pupils. This is creating some discipline problems in the
lowest sets. The teaching styles encouraged are didactic and there is

little teaching material other than books. There is much copying of notes from the board and learning by rote. There have been some modest requests by your colleagues for additional audio-visual materials, but these have been turned down as being something of an extravagance in the present financial climate when there is a shortage of essential books. Requests for the introduction of worksheets have been listened to, but as it has always been the tradition for teachers to prepare their own lessons your head of department feels that individuals should produce their own worksheets.

Matters have come to a head at a departmental meeting when a number of these requests are reiterated by your younger colleagues who are becoming increasingly frustrated and clearly are looking to you for a lead. Your head of department listens to all these complaints with kindly interest and patience, but pleads the current lack of resources as his main excuse for being unable to meet these requests. He is clearly a little irritated when you refer to what happened in your last school. However, he recognises the strength of feeling among the members of your department and eventually proposes a working party to look into all these matters and to present a short report listing priorities to be considered by the whole department. He proposes that you should act as chairman and seeks others who would be prepared to serve on this committee. Two of your lively young colleagues volunteer. You are reminded of the limited financial resources available.

The working party meets and at first tries to decide between the relative merits of particular pieces of new equipment which have been proposed. You soon realise that the real debate is about teaching styles and learning experiences rather than whether an extra slide projector or overhead projector is the top priority. Your younger colleagues have enlightened theories about child development but limited practical experiences as to how these theories can be implemented in classrooms. You recall your fortunate experience at your previous school which arouses considerable interest. Your previous department had been in the middle of a process of curriculum review and consequently had examined closely the nature of teaching learning experiences in your subject at a series of departmental meetings and at a one-day staff seminar. The members of your former department had found this a most rewarding experience, particularly when they had examined together the concepts, skills and attitudes which were involved in a specific unit of work in the subject. They had proceeded to share their ideas and experiences of what they considered to be the appropriate methodology for teaching the various aspects of this unit of work.

The members of your present working party warm to this method of approaching the problem as it seems to grapple with the fundamental issues of what constitutes an effective teaching learning experience. They decide to carry out a limited experiment on similar lines and to offer this to the department as a pilot study of the problems facing the department. This proves to be a time-consuming activity, but you are encouraged by the enthusiasm shown by your colleagues and their readiness to devote time to it.

What becomes apparent as the study proceeds is the variety of learning experiences which are available to the teacher and consequently the complexity of the teacher's task in selecting and managing the variety to seek the experience which is appropriate to a particular learning activity. The three of you decide to try out various experiences during a week's work and above all to seek alternatives to the conventional 'chalk and talk'. One of your colleagues decides to teach the same unit to a class using two different methods and then to seek the views of the pupils as to which method was more effective. Eventually a very different report emerges from that which was originally proposed. Instead of a simple list of priorities in terms of stationery, textbooks and teaching equipment you are able to offer some principles accompanied by some practical examples of how particular learning experiences may be managed by a teacher.

As well as the traditional teaching learning experiences, examples are given of how pupils can be exposed to learning experiences by a variety of stimuli, which may be seen, heard or touched, even smelt or tasted. This may happen either in or out of the school. Interest and curiosity may be aroused and activity motivated in a variety of ways other than simply reading a book, although the latter remains an important stimulus.

When it comes to making recommendations your working party is apprehensive. How far can they go? What are the other members of the department going to say? After all, what you are saying is that each teacher is independent and needs to have access to a wide variety of teaching equipment, and teaching material. It needs to be readily available. A single slide may need to be shown in response to an enquiry. A cumbersome procedure for obtaining and setting up a projector may mean that interest evaporates. A teacher is an opportunist and opportunities for learning may be seized or missed. Several such opportunities may occur during a lesson, each requiring a different strategy and a different treatment. You cannot avoid the conclusion that these activities constitute a composite and complex management exercise. The complexity increases if you add issues such as the layout of the classroom, laboratory or workshop, and the provision of appropriate and adequate resources; all that you have included in the management of the environment.

Not without some anxiety you place your report before the other members of your department.

Questions for discussion

'Preparation' (p.39) *and 'Lesson'* (p.41)

1. How did you prepare for the last day's lessons which you taught? Did your preparation prove to be adequate?
2. What forms of preparation by a teacher may be of a permanent nature and what has to be modified always to meet the needs of a specific class?
3. What can a subject department do to minimise the preparation time which has to be spent by its members?
4. What strategies are available to teachers to ensure a successful beginning and end to a lesson?
5. Discuss the nature of class 'climate'. What are the factors which contribute to it? What characterises a 'climate' in which learning is likely to take place?
6. Discuss recent examples of disruption in lessons and how members of your group have dealt with these. Have any of these been beyond your competence as a class teacher and required the involvement of other members of staff?
7. Draw up a list of essential skills which could be provided during initial training to prepare teachers for classroom management.
8. Discuss which of the following qualities in a teacher are most appreciated by teenage children: teaching skill, discipline, fairness, humour, familiarity, wit, firmness, smart appearance, good looks, leniency, impartiality, personal hygiene. What qualities could be added to this list?
9. Discuss in what ways, if any, relationships between teachers and pupils may be different during out-of-school activities as compared with normal school lessons.
10. Is it possible for interpersonal skills to be taught during the initial or in-service training of teachers or do they have to be learned by experience on the job? Discuss any experience by members of your group of such methods as role play, T groups, transactional analysis etc.
11. If you were an adviser or inspector who had observed the lesson described in the case study what matters would you have discussed with the teacher afterwards?

'Resources' (p.46)

1. Describe the resources which you made use of during a recent lesson. What additional resources would have improved the lesson?
2. What part do you play in the selection and organisation of resources within your department? Are you satisfied with these arrangements or could they be improved?
3. What can be done during the initial training of teachers to prepare them for handling a variety of teaching aids?
4. Discuss the possible ways in which the new technology may influence the development of teaching aids in schools.
5. Discuss the advantages and disadvantages of a central resource centre in a school.
6. Discuss the various systems used for the distribution of the capitation allowance in the schools represented in your group.

'Managing the environment' (p.48)

1. How would you have tackled the problems faced by the teacher in the case study?
2. What features of your present classroom(s) are you dissatisfied with, but over which you have no control?
3. What features have you introduced into your classroom since you started teaching there?
4. Which aspects of your classroom are most important for the teaching of your subject(s)? Which could be improved?
5. Which features of the school environment contribute most to the school's ethos and to the children's learning.
6. Which rituals of school life contribute to the effectiveness of a school's ethos and which are outmoded or out of date?
7. Discuss how particular values are most effectively taught and learned in a school.

'Managing learning experiences' (p.50)

1. What different forms of learning experience did you make use of yesterday in one particular class? Which one was most effective?
2. Which are the most frequent learning experiences used in the teaching of your subject? Which are the most effective? Which require the most preparation beforehand?

3. What can a department do to facilitate the number of different learning experiences available to be used by its members?
4. Is there any value in consulting with pupils as to whether past lessons have been effective? Can pupils contribute to the planning of future lessons?
5. What steps can be taken to give pupils an increased responsibility for their own learning programme?

In-service project work

'Preparation' (p.39) *and 'Lesson'* (p.41)

1. Your head of faculty has suggested that noise levels are too high during lessons. Role play a meeting of members of the faculty at which this matter is discussed.
2. Devise a questionnaire to discover what a group of children thought about one of your lessons. If you are one of a group of teachers following a management course share the results of this enquiry and subsequently discuss what children think makes a good lesson.
3. Work out a programme lasting one term which is aimed at investigating and improving the teaching skills of teachers in a subject department.
4. Accompany a child to his or her lessons for at least one day and encourage colleagues to do likewise. Discuss your findings.

'Resources' (p.46)

1. What can a school do to train its teachers in the use of teaching aids? Outline a programme for a short course which a school might run for its teachers on this topic.
2. Prepare a short slide-tape sequence which might be used to initiate new teachers at your school into the resources which they can make use of; for example, the library, the resource centre, the reprographic services, the school office, the minibus, radio and television, local museums, etc.

'Managing the environment' (p.48)

1. In pairs, role play an interview between the teacher in the case

study and his head of department at which the issues raised by the
case study are discussed.
2. Individually or in groups draw up a list of guidelines which may be
   circularised to teachers in a school in order to improve the school
   environment.
3. Role play in groups or in a plenary session the discussion of one
   such list of guidelines by a department or by a full staff.

'Managing learning experiences' (p.50)

1. In groups of three, role play a meeting of the working party in the
   previous case study. Propose some findings for the report.
2. Role play as a group the departmental meeting at which one of the
   above working party reports is presented.
3. Plan a one day's in-service training programme aimed to raise the
   level of teachers' awareness of variety in learning experiences.
4. Plan a unit of work in your own subject indicating the various
   learning experiences which might be used and the detailed
   teaching methodology which you might use. Explain also what
   resources would be necessary and how much preparation would be
   necessary beforehand. What forms of assessment would you use to
   test the success of the learning experiences?
5. Work out a set of criteria which might be used as part of a staff
   appraisal scheme to assess the performance of a teacher in the
   classroom during a particular lesson?

Chapter 6

Junior Management

In Chapter 4 we made a case for a holistic approach to managing schools, based on the belief that all teachers are managing for learning. The first level of management in these terms is junior management which is concerned with managing learning situations. The activities of teaching and learning, most of which take place in classrooms, laboratories or workshops are the major activities which happen in a secondary school and in exercising responsibility for these activities a teacher is performing a function which is both professional and managerial.

Initial management training

The case studies presented in Chapters 3 and 5 offer examples of junior management and imply the need for class teachers to receive management training. The young probationary teacher in his first teaching post gradually acquired what he described as a 'survival kit' or a series of 'strategies for coping'. He learned the importance of preparing lessons, perhaps as many as twenty or thirty per week depending on the length of individual lessons and the organisation of a timetable. He learned to prepare enough work, but not to attempt too much and to have back-up work available in case the children completed what had been prepared more quickly than expected. He learned to allow time for instructions to be carried out and for questions to be answered. He learned to deal with whole groups of children and not to forget or ignore individual children. He learned to deal with a considerable volume of marking of children's work and to keep records of that marking (p.24). All these tasks, involving preparation and planning, the interpersonal skills of the classroom and simple procedures for assessment, are necessary for a young teacher embarking upon a professional career. They are necessary above all to build confidence and reduce insecurity. The young teacher in our first case study experienced considerable anxiety and reported the symptoms of stress (p.25). Every assistance should be given to young teachers to build their confidence for facing classes of children in secondary schools today. Very positive attitudes of leadership are needed if teachers are to retain the initiative in a teaching and learning situation where the teacher's authority is no longer automatically accepted but has to be earned, and where children are often questioning and sometimes disruptive.

The mastery of a range of skills such as that described above can do much to build the confidence of a young teacher and in our view it is essential that such skills are learned during the period of initial training or at a very early stage in the teacher's career. We go further and assert that this should be a major preoccupation of the initial training period. As to the methods by which these skills are learned during initial training, it is unlikely that they will be acquired by cognitive learning, by reading books or listening to lectures. They are much more likely to be learned by direct practical experience of teaching children which is observed by professional colleagues and which is followed by feedback on their performance. This reference to the importance of the practical element in the initial training of teachers clearly raises questions about the form of that training, which are beyond the scope of this book. However, suffice it to say that we consider the teacher in training to be a management trainee rather than a student teacher. This may help to explain the emphasis which we place on the importance of practising managerial skills while in training.

The professional training of teachers has, for some time, comprised two elements, one academic and the other practical. The academic element has included the study of disciplines such as philosophy, psychology and the history of education. The practical element has been a period or periods of teaching practice in a school. Neither of these elements has included the use of the word 'management'. In fact, teachers have often been somewhat suspicious of 'management' when applied to teaching. The word has only become gradually recognised in the teaching profession when applied to the jobs of Heads, Deputy Heads, heads of department and of others who carry responsibilities other than simply teaching.

This reluctance on the part of teachers to consider their basic job as managerial is an interesting phenomenon. It may be related to the belief that teaching is seen as a vocation and not as a commercial activity. Perhaps one can draw a distinction between the use of the word 'vocation' by other professionals such as doctors or lawyers. Members of the latter professions carry out very personal services for their patients or clients, but those services do not essentially involve getting the patients or clients 'to do something' as an intrinsic part of the service. Recovery from an illness or success in litigation may be considered as a return to a former more 'normal' condition whereas learning always has a sense of development or extension of the learner's knowledge or capabilities. Unless children develop in this way then learning has not taken place. It is in this sense of 'getting something done' (namely learning) by or with other people (namely the learners) that the authors consider teaching to be a managerial activity. Training for such a job is, therefore, not greatly different from being a graduate trainee in other professional or even commercial enterprises in which a strong emphasis on practical experience exists in the training programme.

When one is dealing with an activity which involves the complexity of human development, personal and social values and interpersonal relationships, it is evident that a study of such disciplines as philosophy, psychology and the history of education is relevant and may provide a valuable background to the task of teaching. It is our contention, however, that such academic studies are not the essential priorities required by teachers to teach effectively. Teaching at secondary school level is seldom an academic activity. The knowledge and, even more, the skills needed by teachers to solve initial classroom problems are of a more practical and pragmatic nature and, in our view, may be more readily classified as managerial.

It is interesting to note that while teachers have been reluctant to see themselves as managers, others who perform a not dissimilar task in other spheres have readily adopted the title. In the field of sport, for example, teams have managers. The manager of a football team has a responsibility for teaching players to exercise knowledge and skills. He is concerned that the players develop these skills further and that they perform at their best. He is also concerned with their welfare, an activity which teachers would describe as 'pastoral care'.

Improving managing skills

We have emphasised above that junior management in the teaching profession involves the exercise of practical skills and that these skills are learnt by experience on the job. They are also improved by the same process. It follows that becoming a better teacher is largely a matter of practical experience over what may be a long period of time. Managerial skills are not fully developed during initial training or even during a probationary period in a school. We stress that management training for teachers is not simply providing them with a few 'tricks of the trade' at the outset of their careers, but following up their initial basic training by continued in-service training throughout their careers. This secondary stage may be the responsibility of the school or of a local education authority.

The group of case studies in Chapter 5 illustrate examples of this further development. They concern teachers who have progressed beyond the probationary year of their careers. The initial problems of becoming a teacher have been faced and hopefully overcome, but what our young teacher described in Chapter 3 as 'longer-term anxieties' remain (p.23) well beyond the end of that first year. These anxieties include first and foremost the preparation and planning of a large number of lessons. He or she is provided with a syllabus or scheme of work by the subject department, but soon realises that there is a great gap between this document and what happens in the classroom (p.39). The case study entitled 'Preparation' illustrates the problems of finding time for this crucial task and some of the strategies for overcoming the lack of time (p.40). The subject department can greatly assist all teachers by seeing as part of its role the discussion of the curriculum, not only in terms of what is taught but also in terms of how it is taught. The department or faculty can further help by involving its teachers in the joint preparation of notes, worksheets and other teaching materials, and by developing a workshop approach to preparations (p.40).

Closely related to the preparation of lessons is the management of the learning environment or the setting in which these take place. The case study which illustrates this aspect of management demonstrates how important it is at classroom level, where an environment may be stimulating or stultifying. It also illustrates that the whole school environment has an important influence on children. Corridors, playgrounds, assembly halls,entrance halls and dining rooms by their appearance, contemporary interest, colour, vitality and cleanliness have a silent influence on young people's attitudes and possibly on their behaviour (p.48).

When considering lessons themselves and the management skills which teachers may seek to develop in order to manage learning more effectively in classrooms or in other learning situations, we thought it appropriate to ask the clients what they thought. In many other spheres in which a product or a service is provided it is often thought necessary to seek the views of the customers. We do not claim that we have carried out serious market research, but we have sought the views of a sample of secondary school children on what they thought were the attributes of a good teacher and the characteristics of a good lesson. Nor do we claim that these statements of the children form the sole criteria by which good or bad teaching should be judged, but we do consider that the customers or clients have a legitimate perspective which deserves attention. It was in this spirit that we began with the view of a class teacher in Chapter 1 and when considering the other levels of middle and senior management we again look at the needs of those who are being managed as well as those other needs which may arise from tasks delegated from above.

Some expectations of the learners

At first sight this small sample of young people may not appear to be very demanding of their teachers, nor do their expectations cover a particularly wide range. The enemies of good lessons are boredom and tensions. Boredom develops from repetitive tasks such as copying out notes from a book or a chalkboard, from voices which drone on continuously in the same tone without pauses for questions or discussions and from sitting and writing for long periods. Variety of activity is welcomed in the form of discussion, talking, acting out situations, drawing, watching films or slides and taking part in group work. Tensions arise when teachers are in a bad mood and are not prepared to listen or to help children who are in difficulties. Likewise, resentments develop when children are not treated as human beings but as 'animals' or 'half-wits'. The children seek a relaxed atmosphere in which relationships are characterised by cheerfulness, a sense of humour and a readiness to take a joke. In fact the statements, while seemingly limited in their expectations, focus on two important aspects of teaching and learning, namely the activities which the children engage in and the 'climate' of the classroom in terms of relationships. Looked at a little more closely the expectations are as follows:

1. Teachers are expected to be 'in control' of the classroom situation. A teacher who is not in control is criticised for shouting a lot, threatening pupils with detentions and talking when no one is

listening. Control includes discipline, which most children expect
to be firm, fair and not repressive. Miscreants are dealt with and a
good teacher may be strict, but will not 'take it out on the whole
class'. A classroom becomes disorderly when certain children
assert control. They will quickly take advantage of a teacher who
loses control of a class by being disorganised or unprepared. They
will react to a teacher who is merely repressive or custodial. Their
quotations make it clear that they do not expect to sit still in orderly
rows either listening, doing nothing, or carrying out repetitive
tasks. This implies that teachers have a leadership role in creating
an atmosphere which is conducive to learning. Such an
atmosphere or climate encourages thinking, creativity and activity
rather than passivity and boredom. Control implies motivating the
learners and retaining the initiative.

2. Given a relaxed and positive climate for learning, children expect
to learn from their lessons. When asked questions about good and
bad lessons, the children in our small sample do not refer to
learning as such but they do frequently refer to their 'work'. There
is a tacit understanding that they come to school to work, not
simply to be entertained or to engage in social activity. Children are
sensitive to a 'sloppy' atmosphere when time is being wasted and
lessons are disorganised. They soon recognise when lessons are
unprepared and when a teacher gives them a repetitive task
because he or she 'does not feel like teaching'. They are aware
when a teacher engages in purposeless gossip instead of getting
down to the business of the lesson which is 'work' to them. We
believe that children are often very astute at recognising good
teaching, while perhaps not necessarily knowing why it is good.
They distinguish between teachers, often on a basis of how
effective they are as teachers, and even select optional courses in
secondary schools sometimes not because they prefer the subject,
but because they prefer the teacher and believe they will enjoy
greater success in a subsequent examination having been taught by
that teacher.

3. Young people expect teachers to 'care', particularly in the sense of
caring whether they learn or not. Teachers who are not prepared
to help with difficulties or who are not sensitive to how difficult
some work can be for some children are not seen as good teachers.
Nor are those who are not prepared to explain things or give the
impression that they do not want to be asked questions. We would

be less confident in asserting that children expect teachers to be concerned about their general welfare. Children who are deprived of care in their homes or in their personal lives inevitably appreciate such care from their teachers, but children in need of this kind of help will often select a teacher to approach or in whom to confide. What most children seem to expect of subject teachers is that they should care in the sense of being concerned whether they are succeeding in learning what they are being taught. This means knowing where they are in their learning programme, answering their questions, helping them over their difficulties and taking time to explain what has not at first been understood. All this implies that learning needs to be individualised by a teacher. Whether or not there is mixed ability teaching in a class, there is always mixed ability learning.

4. Increasingly, young people in secondary schools appreciate the opportunity to share in planning and evaluating their own learning programmes. We cannot say they expect this to happen because it is still a very rare occurrence. Nevertheless, it is not unreasonable to recognise that the customers have a legitimate perspective on their own learning just as we recognise that our sample of young people make reasonable and perceptive statements about good and bad lessons. They will have views on why their learning has not been successful and how teaching might be rendered more effective. This means providing opportunities for young people to comment on what they are learning; for example, whether they consider it relevant or whether it seems 'to have nothing to do with life when you leave school'. They may also have pertinent comments to make on how they are learning, and this implies an open climate in which they can express views and opinions not only upon the content of lessons but upon the methods of teaching being used. This form of interchange on the quality of teaching may pose a considerable threat to some teachers. Nevertheless, such consultations have become accepted practice in certain countries, notably in Scandinavia, and we believe this trend will spread more widely. Negotiation is one of the skills of management which is becoming increasingly necessary at all levels and it will be essential if and when teachers and learners negotiate the learning agenda.

If these are some of the expectations which young people have of their teachers, can we analyse some of the knowledge, skills and strategies which are required of teachers if they are to meet these expectations?

The skills of junior management

If teachers are to be 'in control' of the teaching situation there is a clear need for planning and preparation. This process goes back first to the learning environment and to the creation of the physical conditions which determine the climate. In the case study on managing the learning environment (pp.48-50) the teacher tackles the improvement of the classroom by various initiatives, to convert an unpromising situation not only by brightening it up, but ensuring that teaching materials and teaching aids are readily available. The furniture is rearranged and he then sets about the task of distributing the equipment held in a central store around to the members of the department, thus allowing each member to be more independent (p.50).

Lessons clearly need to be planned and prepared beforehand. Once a teacher is committed to a programme of lessons for a school year, the demands on his or her time far exceed those of a limited period of teaching practice. The teacher in the case study entitled 'Preparation' is keenly aware of this problem and considers a variety of strategies for converting the bare bones of the syllabus into schemes of work and into lesson plans (pp.39-41). He considers what he is going to do and what the children are going to do. Not all lessons can be given the same degree of detailed preparation. Certain 'key' lessons or 'master' lessons will serve as 'cairns' to chart a way through a scheme of work and to teach the major ideas, concepts or skills which feature in the syllabus. These lessons will require very careful and detailed preparation and they will be modified and improved after they have taken place in the light of experience. If these can be observed by colleagues and later discussed within a subject department the work of that department will be strengthened and the confidence of its teachers progressively built up.

Resources and teaching materials need to be organised and prepared beforehand. These may range from the simple provision of an adequate number of textbooks to the complexities of equipment and apparatus required for lessons in Science, Art or Craft. Any form of individualised learning requires even more meticulous attention to detail, for in these circumstances learners require individual

assignments, corresponding worksheets and possibly tools or kits of
equipment. Banks of resources need to be stored in such a way that
they are readily available and can be simply retrieved. The teacher in
our case study introduces what he describes as 'a somewhat
ramshackle retrieval system' but it works. Materials are readily
available for the children (p.50). Modern teaching methods require a
far greater degree of preparation and a skill in the management of
resources than was the case when a textbook and a piece of chalk were
thought sufficient. The use of a variety of audio-visual teaching
techniques may improve the quality of teaching in many subjects, but
such techniques need to be mastered beforehand. The case study
illustrates this clearly (p.46-47). When their pupils are daily
acquainted with the sophisticated offerings of the media, teachers
cannot afford to present notes or transparencies for an overhead
projector which are illegible or get slides in a projector either upside
down or back to front. The survey by H.M.I. entitled 'Aspects of
Secondary Education in England' (1979) painted a somewhat grey
picture of the methodology used in many secondary schools, where
'chalk and talk' remained the stock in trade of many teachers. The
improvements needed imply an increase in managerial skills applied
at the preparatory stage in, for example, the professional production
of documentation such as notes, worksheets or transparencies for the
overhead projector. This has implications not only for the individual
teacher but, as the case study 'Resources' suggests, becomes a matter
for training at department or at school level (p.47).

The second expectation of learners, namely that they should learn
from their lessons, has implications in the field of organisation and
human relationships. It is important to stress the active nature of
learning once again in this context and the fact that most learning
takes place when learners 'do something'. Passivity is rarely an
appropriate state of mind or body for effective learning. If activity is
to take place in a lesson, then the situation needs to be managed. A
teacher needs to have a clear idea of what he or she is going to do and
of what the learners are going to do. Learners then need to be
motivated to engage in the activity which has been planned. We have
already drawn a broad distinction between those activities and
strategies which are preparatory to learning and those which take
place in the learning situation. The two case studies reveal the
distinction between the preparation and lesson itself (pp.39-43). To
pursue the imagery of the theatre, once the curtain is up and the
performance is on, there is seldom much opportunity for further

preparation or planning. Once in the classroom, laboratory, or workshop, a teacher needs to keep the performance going. The skills involved in sustaining a lesson which has been appropriately well prepared lie mainly in the field of interpersonal relationships. The teacher in the case study 'Lessons' has a problem in relationships when deciding to deal with the drawing on the chalkboard in a peremptory and sarcastic manner rather than to treat it with lighthearted humour. Once into the lesson the teacher is now leading and managing people. However, this is not simply a matter of telling children what to do. Teaching involves a repertoire of interpersonal skills such as encouraging, persuading, communicating and supporting. Teachers are called upon to act as enablers, facilitators and consultants. It is necessary sometimes to mediate or arbitrate between a group of learners in the event of conflict.

In addition to these human skills there is also an element of organisation which is essential to a successful lesson. The lesson needs to be structured to facilitate learning and while this implies careful preparation, it also involves successful implementation of what has been planned. At a simple level there needs to be a beginning, a middle and an end. The example from the case study quoted above illustrates the importance of an effective start to a lesson and the same case study shows how a lesson can end very untidily, with children not hearing instructions for homework clearly in their rush to leave the classroom. A lesson needs to link effectively with a previous lesson. Opportunities need to be found for practice or exercise of what has been taught, but lengthy practice should not be simply a means of filling in time. The ends of lessons are important in that adequate time is necessary for clearing-up, particularly in practical subjects where there are tools and other equipment to be stored away in an orderly fashion and work areas to be cleaned.

The third expectation of learners is that teachers should 'care' whether they learn or not and such expectations are effectively met by appropriate monitoring, assessment and evaluating of what learning has taken place. Care in this sense is not a general concern for the learners' welfare, nor even making appreciative noises or superficially critical comments. What we have in mind is again very practical and managerial rather than emotional. It implies appropriate processes of monitoring, which may simply be in the form of questions to check what has been learned or may extend to much more formal assessment in the form of testing and examining. When such assessment has taken place, records need to be kept and reports may need to be written. Schools often develop systems for such reporting processes or for more extended profiles of children, but individual teachers still need to develop effective means of knowing where their pupils 'are' in the learning process. It is inadequate simply to record that learners have encountered the various elements in a syllabus. The fact that a teacher has taught something is no guarantee that all children have learned it. A teacher must seek evidence that children can handle ideas, or successfully practise skills. Children also need to know what they have learned, because knowledge of achievement is a powerful stimulus to further learning. Teachers need an understanding of such techniques as criterion-referenced assessment in order to reinforce success and not imbue learners with a sense of failure.

Finally, if we acknowledge the expectation of learners at secondary school level to be involved with their teachers in negotiating their learning programme, then those teachers will be called upon to exercise a further repertoire of human skills which we could describe as managerial and which come under the general heading of 'consultation'. The first stage in this process is for teachers to listen to learners, prompting and encouraging them to talk about themselves and their learning needs. Learners need to be encouraged to reflect upon their past learning experiences and to comment frankly and openly upon such experiences. Such interchanges of perspectives on a learning experience demand considerable managerial skill on the part of a teacher. Those teachers who have been accustomed to adopt the magisterial stance of 'teacher knows best' may well find the learning of such skills a somewhat painful process which poses a threat to their self-esteem and self-confidence. However, once they are able to develop the skills of listening and accepting criticism and then proceed to build constructively and positively an agenda for learning, they will extend what may be described as the 'comfort zone' of both teachers and learners, thus creating a more open climate and enhancing the possibilities of learning. It must be emphasised, though, that negotiation and consultation are managerial skills which need to be learned in practice and do not simply come naturally. In fact, they represent a group of skills which have not traditionally been expected of teachers who have a reputation for talking rather than listening and telling rather than discussing.

A summary of junior management skills

It may be helpful to summarise those managerial skills which, in our view, are necessary as essential priorities if teachers are to cope effectively in classrooms and enable learning to take place.

1. Planning and preparation: the development of schemes of work and lesson plans from syllabuses, the detailed preparation of 'key' or 'master' lessons and the provision of 'follow-up' lessons. Target setting.

2. Resource organisation: the provision of teaching materials, equipment, documentation and apparatus, the mastery of teaching aids, the organisation of time and space.

3. Interpersonal relationships: communicating, counselling, consulting, negotiating, motivating, arbitrating, listening, confidence-building, group dynamics and individual interviewing.

4. Monitoring, assessment and evaluation including self-evaluation, record-keeping, testing, examining, report writing and profiling.

5. Leadership: although an aspect of interpersonal relationships, leadership is mentioned separately as a necessary managerial skill in the classroom; it means involving and gaining the commitment of learners to the tasks of learning. A teacher is always performing the role of a change agent because learning changes people.

It is surely strange that, when asked, teachers see leadership in schools in terms of Heads and senior staff. They equate status, authority and power with leadership, and are generally unwilling to see themselves as the real leaders. If the work of a school is carried out by students, then those who define that work, organise it and arrange for its completion and assessment can be described as leaders. Whether anything happens depends upon them. The leadership of groups of young people is a crucial skill and to exercise it effectively needs a blending of certain skills of management. These include motivation and the setting of targets. Increasingly, the style of leadership is that of discussion, consultation, participation and negotiation. The fact that teachers have little experience of the exercise of these skills in the school professional community may be one reason why they do not seek to develop this climate in their classrooms.

The summary of topics given above can form the basis of in-service training in junior management which can be carried out in a

The summary of topics given above can form the basis of in-service training in junior management which can be carried out in a secondary school and may form part of a staff development programme for the whole school or for individual subject departments. A typical unit of such a training programme might include case studies such as those in the previous chapter followed by discussion in groups, talks by practising teachers on relevant topics and a significant practical element. Once again we emphasise that skills are acquired in practice. In the case of preparation and assessment this may take the form of workshop sessions. The practice of interpersonal skills can only take place in real classroom situations when there is observation by a skilled practitioner and feedback on performance provided for the learner. This is a method of improving teaching skills which we hope will become accepted as perfectly normal by the teaching profession, whether or not it is associated with appraisal and related to promotion or financial rewards. Before being introduced as a means of training into a school or a subject department the method needs to be fully discussed and criteria worked out. Colleagues who are to observe each other need to agree beforehand what is to be observed. Subsequent discussion is best carried out on a one-to-one basis rather than in a group situation which may be somewhat threatening for the learner. Some schools find it helpful to design a proforma for use by observers and a considerable amount of literature is now available on the subject of classroom observation.

We are anxious to reiterate that these skills of junior management do not constitute the whole business of teaching. The particular type of rapport which is established between teacher and learner, the imagination required to build images, construct examples and make analogies, the capacity to use metaphor and simile, the understanding of the society of the classroom, and the psychology of human development are some of the elements which contribute to effective teaching over and above the mastery of content and subject matter. However, what we seek to show is that the list of managerial skills given above is an essential prerequisite of effective teaching and learning. They are skills which are attributed to managers everywhere.

Suggestions for further reading

BARNES, D. (1971) *Language, the learner and the school* (London, Penguin).

BARNES, D. (1977) *From communication to curriculum* (London, Penguin).

BESWICK, N. (1977) *Resource-based learning* (London, Heinemann Educational).

CASSIDY, A., HUSTLER, D. and CUFF, E. (1986) *Action-research in schools* (London, Allen and Unwin).

ELLIOTT, J. (1981) *Action Research – a framework for self-evaluation in schools,* mimeo (Cambridge Institute of Education).

HARGREAVES, D.N. (1967) *Social relations in a secondary school* (London, Routledge and Kegan Paul).

HOUSE E., and LAPAN, S. (1978) *Survival in the Classroom* (Boston, Allyn and Bacon).

KEMMIS, S. *et al* (1981) *The Action-Research Planner* (Deakin University, Australia).

MARLAND, M. (1975) *The Craft of the Classroom: a survival guide* (London, Heinemann Educational).

OPEN UNIVERSITY (1981) *Observing Classroom Processes* (E. 364 Block 3) The Open University, Milton Keynes.

PAYNE, G. and CUFF, T. (1982) *Doing Teaching: the practical management of classrooms* (London, Batsford).

RICHARDSON, E. (1973) *The Environment of Learning* (London, Heinemann Educational).

STUBBS, M. and DELAMONT, S. (1976) *Explorations in Classroom Observation* (Chichester, Wiley).

WALKER, R. and ADELMAN, C. (1975) *A Guide to Classroom Observation* (London, Methuen).

Chapter 7

Case Studies: Middle Management

1. Sharing: a department pools its talents

Older staffroom colleagues will sometimes, without the need for too
much prompting, tell of the days when all staff, or at least, all senior
staff, had their very own chair in the staffroom, and of the trouble that
followed when an unsuspecting junior sat in the wrong place. Such
practices, though the basis of much folklore, have little current
existence, but it is not unusual for particular groups of staff to
congregate in a particular part of the staffroom on a regular basis.
Such groups may be created by a shared activity, like bridge, or an
interest, like sport, or may, especially in a large staff, be familiarity
groups, largely or exclusively made up of the members of a particular
department.

So it is today, and indeed it was yesterday, and probably will be
tomorrow, that you find yourself surrounded by departmental
colleagues as you take your well-earned cup of coffee at morning
break. The conversation ranges widely, but is suddenly focused by a
remark from one of the gathering that the quality of some of the
school-produced teaching material in use by the department in the
second year is so poor as to be embarrassing. This remark uncorks a
general dissatisfaction from all directions, involving the inadequate
supplies and state of repair of textbooks and equipment, the range
and quality of work-booklets generally, and the widespread
duplication of effort which results when each teacher of the subject is
preparing his or her own material for each class.

Already aware that very often even the most passionate debates
over coffee dissipate like steam when each goes off to their next
encounter, you venture to suggest that you would take a critical look at
the second-year work-booklet, and come up with some suggested
improvements, if others would find this useful. The head of
department, seizing on your offer with ill-disguised haste, asks
around your colleagues to see if there are others who will undertake a

similar operation with other years, and gets some volunteers. He
suggests that about two weeks should be sufficient for an initial review,
and then proposes to call a departmental meeting to assess progress,
and to decide on subsequent action.

You finish your coffee, collect your books and your thoughts, and
move off in search of your next class. As you do so, you wonder about
the common sense of your offer. It is true that you have wanted to
radically alter the second-year work-book, and indeed, that you have
not really made much use of it recently because it seems so
inadequate. But modifying for yourself is one thing, redesigning it for
all in the department is another. The action of the head of department
has made such a move legitimate, for to have rewritten the booklet
without official encouragement would have risked the disapproval of
colleagues who might see such action as presumptuous. Others would
be engaged in a similar task, and so would both help you and
appreciate the nature of the task, thus making them more
sympathetic to your efforts. And, if the process goes well, you can
have the personal satisfaction of knowing that your work has helped
many more students than you yourself teach, as well as your
colleagues. You cannot help feeling apprehensive, however, at the
task you have taken on. At least, though, you can take for granted the
support and help of your head of department, who was clearly very
pleased that you agreed to have a go.

2. Interruptions: what are the priorities? Learning or administration?

You cannot deny that the prospect of taking 3R always makes you a
little nervous. It is not that they have a reputation for being a badly
behaved group, but rather that their lessons are difficult to predict.
On occasions, they respond very well indeed to the topic of the day,
and obviously enjoy their work, but there have been times when they
have never really become engaged in the lesson, and then they have
the capacity to be positively unruly. Today, however, things are going
well. The mood is purposeful, there is a readiness to join in, and a very
lively discussion is proceeding. Even the self-appointed class cynic has
left his mask aside, and has committed himself to a strongly held point
of view. You are enjoying the sense of well-being that accompanies the
learning process.

At that moment, the door opens and your head of department
comes in, apologising to both you and the class for the interruption,

and indicating that he wants a brief word with you. The class is left in the air, with the unfinished discussion subsiding all around, and their resentment is quickly made evident by being translated into their own private debates; a steeply rising volume of noise results. When aware that this state of affairs not only prevents your head of department's words from being clearly heard, but also reflects adversely on your reputation for class control, you demand a state of silent suspended animation; this lasts for a few moments and then breaks down. In desperation you set a hastily conceived piece of written work that fits only marginally into the structure of the lesson, and turn to listen once more to your head of department.

He repeats his regret at having to interrupt your lesson, and goes on to explain his reasons for it. It seems that the Deputy Head in charge of external examinations is chasing him to present the lists of the entry for GCSE, all in alphabetical order, and has set a deadline of 4 p.m. that day. He regrets the short notice that he has been given by the Deputy and you wonder whether this is true or whether he has simply forgotten, and is trying to put the blame on senior management. Just as these thoughts are going through your mind, he reminds you that he had mentioned the need for the entry lists at a departmental meeting three months ago. Before you have a chance to respond, assuming that you have a reply to hand, he hurriedly departs, once more regretting the intrusion, and apologising to the class, who have been going through the motions of the written exercise, while straining to hear the conversation between the staff.

As the door closes you wrestle with the temptation to ask the class to continue with the written work. You argue to yourself that this will prevent yet another disruption of the lesson, and doubt whether you can revive the discussion that was going so well. You know only too well that to do so would give you time to prepare the lists immediately, and so leave the lunch hour clear, and you know that to do so would be selling the present class short. You stop the written exercise, promise to return to it some time in the future, and start to get the lesson back to the earlier discussion. You also work out in your mind how, by rushing lunch, you can do the lists, and attend a meeting of the students interested in a skiing holiday next year.

3. Spending: who decides how the money is spent?

Making your way along the corridor towards the staffroom in search of a cup of coffee at break one day just after Easter, you see your head of faculty deep in conversation with a colleague. As you pass, she looks up, pauses in her conversation, greets you with a cheery comment, and explains that she was hoping to see you as she has a list she has just received from the Deputy Head in charge of Resources. She thrusts the typewritten sheet into your hand, threatening the stability of a large pile of exercise books you are carrying under the other arm, and you see that it is covered with a mass of figures relating to the distribution of the new financial year's capitation allowances. It is only possible to obtain a very general and confusing impression of what you see, and you are about to seek some clarification of these figures when she asks you for your suggestions as to what requirements you have for books and materials for your classes. She explains that she needs details in the next few days so that she can put together the faculty requisition to ensure that orders are placed in time to enable deliveries to be made before the start of the September term.

She is just about to move off down the corridor when you begin to articulate some of the many questions that are beginning to form in your mind. You ask her in what form does she want the information, and she replies that a simple list will do. You ask her how much money is available to you, and she tells you with a smile that there is not enough, but ask for what you want, and she will sort out how much you can spend when she has all the lists in from your faculty colleagues. She has begun to walk away to find another member of staff when you enquire loudly whether reference books are to be included and she shouts back over her shoulder that these are ordered via the Library requisition and can wait until a later date.

You are confused. You are pleased to have been asked to play a part in determining how the faculty's capitation is spent, but you are far from clear as to how much of a say you have, and how to go about saying it. If you were to present too long and expensive a list, it could look greedy and unrealistic. If the list is too short it will be seen that you lack ideas and are too easily satisfied. Yet what constitutes a reasonable length? If too much detail is included from the catalogues the list may look fussy, as well as take too much time to prepare. Too little detail may mean that you either have to repeat the exercise, or miss out on items that the head of faculty would have ordered if they had been properly identified. More important than the compiling of lists are the judgements needed to choose suitable items. It was flattering to be asked, but have you the experience to decide wisely about suitable textbooks, quantities of materials, and to resolve the competing claims of the various publishers and suppliers? Where could inspection copies and examples be viewed? And to what extent was it necessary to have a common approach to purchasing on behalf of the whole faculty?

You have so many questions to be answered that you proceed in the quest for a coffee and a colleague who can provide at least some of the answers you need. You also begin to see the value of a faculty meeting to discuss the requisition, and the nature of at least part of the role of the head of faculty.

4. Meeting (1): chairing a departmental meeting

It is soon after the beginning of the summer term, and there has been a note in your pigeon-hole in the letter rack announcing that there is to be a full meeting of the department after school today. So ten minutes after the final bell sees you sitting around a small table in the head of department's classroom, waiting for all your colleagues to assemble. The waiting is rather protracted, as two colleagues are delayed on bus duty, and then a search is instituted that discovers a third sitting in the staffroom drinking coffee, having forgotten all about the meeting. Even a reminder in the weekly staff bulletin has not ensured a prompt and full attendance. When another member announces before the meeting starts that he must leave in an hour, as he is accompanying a theatre visit by the senior students, you doubt whether the meeting is going to achieve anything except heightened exasperations and irritability.

However, having resolved the problem of getting a busy, and less than fully efficient staff together, the head of department outlines the agenda, previously circulated with the notice for the meeting. The main topics are the determination of teaching groups for next year, along with which staff it is hoped will teach each group. Also to be discussed are room bases, and the allocation of teaching materials. She goes on to indicate the existing policy of the department as regards fixing the size and composition of the teaching groups, suggests the limits that constrain any proposed policy changes and sketches some alternative ideas for the creation of sets.

The silence that greets the conclusion of her opening remarks is short lived. Your own ideas take some time to formulate, but there are several others keen to voice their own thoughts on the method to be used. At first, it seems that everyone present has an original approach and there is little common ground. In response to questions about the practical difficulties of implementing some of the notions, the head of department manages to establish two main strategies, and asks which is the more acceptable. Further discussion begins to lead in the direction of one of these, and the meeting agrees to try that approach this year, with the clear understanding that it will be reviewed in the light of experience, and if it is not working well, the other method will be tried next year.

The eagerness to offer ideas about the methods of arriving at the setting is in contast to the diffidence that greets the head of department's enquiry about who would like to teach which class. There is so little comment that she suggests that she will speak individually with each member of the department over the next week, compile a list of preferences, arbitrate where there is conflict, and present the resulting list to the timetable team with the hope that their efforts will bear some resemblance to the original. Preferences over which room will form each member of staff's base are expressed with great readiness, bordering on vehemence in several cases. Arguments range from stockroom facilities to the suitability of rooms as tutor group bases. Territorial rights are clearly of great importance. The head of department listens, as she does over the distribution of teaching materials, and without pressing for a neat conclusion at what is fast approaching the time agreed beforehand for the close of the meeting, tells everyone that she will write up a brief account of the discussions together with her allocation of rooms and resources. She invites colleagues to make any observations when they see her about which teaching groups they are to have. Then everyone will receive a copy of the modified list before it goes into the timetabling process.

You have not managed to say a lot during the meeting, but you collect your coat and the night's marking. As you drive home you reflect, as you have done on many previous occasions, that what had begun as a somewhat confused gathering, at the end of a hectic day had developed into a useful exchange of ideas and information. This owes a great deal to the skills of chairmanship possessed by the head of department.

5. Meeting (2): problems emerge in an informal gathering. Seeking joint solutions

The parents' evening has seemed never-ending. You began your interviews just after 6.30 p.m. and although two sets of parents have not yet been to see you, you are having your last arranged appointment. The parents listen intently to your words about their daughter, largely agree with your comments, ask about the prospects for her if she chooses to continue certain subjects and rise to leave. You notice that the clock at the back of the hall shows 9.55 p.m. The missed appointments should have taken place an hour ago and you look around, hoping that perhaps these parents did not arrive after all. There is no one who seems to be waiting to see you and so you collect together your work-books and papers, and prepare to leave. Most of your fellow tutors are finishing also and you see the caretaker hovering by the door, ready to lock up the school. You take your possessions to the staffroom, put them into your locker, and return to the entrance hall to join your tutor colleagues for a welcome drink.

In the pub, after exchanging stories about the various encounters during the evening, the conversation centres on the current atmosphere prevailing amongst the year group. Several of your colleagues begin to express disquiet about aspects of their behaviour, and this quickly broadens into more general dissatisfaction. Observations about the noise levels when the year assembles lead to comments about the lack of attention of one particular group of boys during the hymns. Another colleague asks if others share the view that when they are moving along corridors, waiting to enter classrooms, or leaving at the end of the day, they seem intent on the maximum disturbance. Litter in the part of the school designated for them to spend their breaks and lunch hour has become most noticeable, and several parents have commented this evening about disruptions during lessons that have interrupted their particular child's concentration. A member of the Physical Education staff tells of the difficulties being experienced in getting a full commitment to school teams, and others say there is a widespread reluctance to take part in extra-curricular activities. Some colleagues even talk of rebelliousness and alienation creeping in.

The conversation then moves on to causes, and several persuasive but partial analyses are offered, from impending unemployment to lack of rigour in applying a code of discipline, via parental attitudes and the influence of television. Then the first hiatus occurs when someone asks what can be done to change things for the better, especially by the tutors, whose readiness to show concern over the situation seems evidence that they would want to do something practical to bring about an improvement. General ideas begin to emerge, but it is not until the landlord calls time that the head of year, present but quiet throughout the whole conversation, ventures an opinion.

He welcomes the evident concern, agrees with much of the explanation offered, and sounds very pleased indeed at the tentative offerings of specific help. He particularly draws the group's attention to the fact that, acting together, there is a good prospect of influencing the mood of the year, while each operating on their own will have little impact. He accepts, without being asked to, some of the blame for the present state of affairs, and, just as the occasion is brought to an end at the landlord's insistence, he volunteers to put the gist of the conversation down on paper, outline a programme of action, and have the whole issue discussed at a meeting of year tutors this week, before showing the whole thing to senior management for their comments and support.

6. Developing: a staff development interview

You are very well aware that ever since you began teaching you have been assisted at all times by the friendly advice and example of your fellow professionals and have valued the frequent informal occasions when you have enquired about school procedures, classroom techniques, professional behaviour and a host of other details. On some matters, a chance remark has led to a long discussion, developed over a drink, or continued at home when a colleague has been invited with the idea of exploring his attitude to your applying for a new job. In addition to these experiences, however, you also take part in the school's formal staff-development programme, and the time of year when this is held is fast approaching. Your head of department saw you in the staffroom last week and you both agreed that after school today would be a good time to hold the discussion and you have prepared some ideas to consider at this meeting. You are anxious, yet looking forward to it. It is unlikely to be without its difficult moments, and you may even feel positively uncomfortable about some things, but, in essence, you anticipate with pleasure the very flattering prospect of a half-hour conversation about yourself.

She greets you warmly, and clearly seems to be looking forward to the meeting also, and, after making sure that the coffee is all right, she begins by asking you to talk about your perceptions of the teaching experiences of the past year. You describe the classes you have had, and expand a little on the way each has had a different identity, presented different problems, and achieved different successes. She enquires about those aspects of teaching these classes that you feel you now do better than before, and what you consider to be your continuing or even newly found weaknesses. You talk at length about the difficulty of achieving an improvement in interaction amongst certain groups and she comments very favourably about the obvious enthusiasm that one particular third-year class is now showing. She taught them last year, and has recently, during a day's absence of yours, found herself taking them again. They have left her in no doubt that they are enjoying the work. She asks you for your candid opinion about the immediate and long-term goals of the faculty, and encourages your comments on the general tone of the school. After twenty minutes your initial reserve has been replaced by confidence and you hear yourself saying things that you have often thought, but had not intended to raise at the discussion. You even ask for her help in trying to think of ways of establishing better relations with a colleague whose manner and philosophy you cannot stand or understand.

Then the conversation moves to considering your longer-term future in the profession, including the advisability of your seeking promotion in another school. She does not rule this out, but adds other strategies that will extend your experiences, including visits to other schools, an in-service course run by the Authority and teaching new classes next year. The relaxed and friendly mood of the encounter does not prevent the issues from being clearly and crisply presented and you grow as a professional by seeing yourself through other eyes. That this is so is due to the respect you have for her professionalism, the fact that you know that she has seen you teach and can assess your worth, and that she evidently has your interests at heart.

7. Helping: support in a crisis

When you first began to teach the class, you were hardly aware that she was there. After a while you formed an impression of her as a hard-working, polite and rather shy girl, whose attendance was good, and who always kept up-to-date with her work. Then, without any apparent cause, a few weeks ago she failed to hand in a piece of homework, and when you tackled her about this, she simply blushed, apologised and promised not to make the same mistake again, but did not volunteer any sort of explanation. As this was the first time, you took no further action, and when she found you the next day to hand the work to you, you were reassured that this was a momentary lapse. It is true, that, looking back, you had noticed that she seemed more than usually preoccupied in class from time to time, but all this had in no way prepared you for the events of the lesson today. The class had been working for about twenty minutes and the written exercise they were doing was nearing completion when, as you were moving amongst the desks, you noticed that, unlike all the others, she had written only three lines, and was staring out of the window.

You stopped to question her, in a tone of surprise and some annoyance, whereupon she put her pen down with some force upon the desk and, going bright red, and in a rapidly rising voice, she shouted that she thought the work was a complete waste of her time and everyone else's and, what was more, you were picking on her again. The rest of the class stopped instantly, and watched, hardly seeming to breathe, as she stood up from her desk and, before you could recover yourself sufficiently to speak, marched out.

For a moment you hesitated and then followed her into the corridor, leaving a stunned class to regain its collective voice. As you entered the corridor you just had time to see her enter the toilets. You paused, reflected and then decided to go back to your class. You then sent one of the students to ask the head of her year if he could come to your classroom. You tried to get the class to behave as if nothing had happened. They are clearly upset, especially two or three girls who are friendly with her, and offer to go in search of her to bring her back. You thank them, but decline their offer, saying that the head of year will deal with it. When he arrives you quickly tell him of the outburst and he goes in pursuit.

After the lesson is over, you make your way to the head of year's office and find him and the girl deep in conversation. You apologise for the interruption and go away again, so that it is some hours later that you are again free to go to the head of year and ask about the girl. He asks you to sit down and smiles when you enquire whether this is an isolated incident directed against you personally, or whether other staff have had the same experience. Does he think that you caused the outburst and that you victimised her, or was it a case of you being the unlucky one who just happened to trigger off this reaction? You need to know whether you did the right thing by not pursuing her to the toilets, and by sending for the head of year, and how to prevent it happening again. You need to know how to begin to rebuild a broken relationship with the girl, and how to cope with her re-entry into the class situation. In your anxiety to know how to cope, you hardly give the head of year the chance to explain the set of home pressures caused by a serious illness to her mother and then a row with her boyfriend that has led to the outburst today, or even that the girl had been asking how to go about apologising because she likes you as a teacher and now feels ashamed of what she has done.

Questions for discussions

1. Do teachers benefit from working in teams? Why?
2. Do teams need designated heads? If so, do these have to be permanent? Can they be:
    (a) temporary;
    (b) elected;
    (c) rotating?
3. What functions usually undertaken by heads of departments or by heads of years could be better left to teachers?
4. Are administrative tasks the proper use of the time and expertise of the more highly paid?
5. Would you see merit in using the money presently paid as a head of department or year allowance to engage a secretary to the team?
6. Consider your reaction to the following suggestions:
    (a) Holding a team meeting specifically to examine and evaluate the role of the team leader.
    (b) Inviting each team member to chair meetings in turn.
    (c) The team should prepare an annual report on the work of the team, and its leader.
7. What is the worth of holding meetings of heads of departments or heads of years? Are these for mutual support, to gain power from more senior management or to divert attention from the real issues?
8. Are middle managers born or can they be trained?
9. If you are a middle manager:
    (a) What methods do you employ to find out the true feelings about your leadership amongst members of your team?
    (b) How do you measure your effectiveness?
    (c) How are you preparing your successor?
    (d) Have you more in common with others on the same scale or with the same title, or with colleagues in the same team?
    (e) How do you want senior management to treat you? Is this how you treat your team?
10. If you have a middle manager responsible for you:
    (a) Does this person command your respect? Why or why not?
    (b) Do you want the job some day? Why?
    (c) Would you do the job differently? Why?
    (d) Does your manager know what you think?
    (e) How could your manager be of more help to you and how

might you be managed more effectively?
11. What tasks in schools can teams engage in more effectively than individuals?
12. How effective are management courses for middle managers? Share your experiences of such courses.

In-service project work

1. Work out in your group a set of criteria which might be used to appraise a head of department or a head of year. Who should carry out this appraisal?
2. Outline a management course for middle managers in secondary schools, indicating the duration, course content and methods of learning to be used.
3. Role play in pairs a staff development interview similar to the one outlined in the case study on page 80.

Chapter 8

Middle Management

The situations described in the previous chapter depict the 'middle manager' at work in a school. The term has gained general acceptance in recent years, at least in so far as it is widely used. We aim to examine the concept of middle management from the point of view of teachers and so to establish whether or not there is real justification for the existence of such roles. In doing so, however, it may be helpful to begin by reviewing the more traditionally held views about such posts.

The traditional view of middle management in secondary schools

Looking at the structure and organisation of a school from the Head's chair, it seems entirely logical to arrange for the designation of a number of staff as middle managers. It is true that this did not occur formally in secondary schools when these were small, relatively simple and, above all, stable institutions; the head of department, for instance, was only recognised by the Burnham Committee for salary purposes in 1954, and subsequently abolished by the same Committee in 1971! The Head appointed to a growing school, often in the throes of reorganisation, and with increasing pressures on him was, and still is, glad enough to depute to others a share in the running of the school. Generally, however, these matters so delegated are the ones that are least likely to be mis-handled, or, if they are, have less serious consequences. Authority to carry out roles such as head of department or faculty, house or year has been seen as emanating from the Head, who has taken a major role in such appointments, has determined job specifications where they exist and has made such post-holders accountable to the senior management of the school. Often such posts have been a device for control and communication enabling Heads and their Deputies to relate to a small number of people who can, in turn, reach the whole staff. Thus such appointments have aided the Head's span of control and lightened the physical load.

A second advantage to the Head of creating middle managers has been that they have harnessed the particular knowledge of subject specialists, especially important at a time when syllabuses, work-schemes, texts and methods of teaching have all been undergoing rapid, even violent, change. Each senior member of staff has but partial knowledge of the secondary school curriculum from first-hand experience and cannot claim to have a grasp of the detail of each discipline. It has been expedient, therefore, to delegate such matters as choice of syllabus, ordering of materials, classroom equipment and layout, and even the grouping of pupils to 'experts', or at least to seek their advice before taking decisions. In so far as this has happened, it is not unusual for the head of the department responsible for the Head's own specialist field to complain that, while others have a free hand, or are at least consulted, the Head makes the decisions in those areas familiar to him.

However, some delegation to less senior colleagues has been motivated by the desire on the part of some Heads to begin extending the range of an individual's responsibility and administrative experience with a view to preparing for future senior management. Proven competence in extra-curricular activities has often contributed to enhanced promotion prospects. In addition, to be singled out for extra work, far from being resented by the person concerned, has been much sought after because of the status, improved prospects and extra rewards thus available. To those selected for a middle management role, their worth recognised by tangible means, the result has been improved morale and, with a plentiful supply of points when schools were growing and a highly mobile teaching force, resentment amongst those not chosen has been of little lasting consequence – almost everyone could console themselves that their time was not far off, or would keep quiet for fear of harming their own references or promotion prospects. Conditions have changed. With falling school rolls, fewer points and a much less mobile teaching force, the effects on staff morale of the creation of a middle management tier have changed too. It has become especially difficult for some teachers who, denied promotion themselves, witness those who received it in the years of expansion doing little or nothing to justify the extra rewards. Undoubtedly, some were promoted with few qualities that are now apparent and to posts sometimes of dubious validity.

If the prime motivation for the establishing of posts of responsibility has been to share out the tasks of running the school from the Head to colleagues, the post-holders have been accountable to him, accredited and authorised by him. Any such job evaluation relies on the Head expressing his estimate of the way his tasks have been performed by others; it has been his assessment that is the valid one. It is hardly surprising, therefore, that many staff have been less ready than Heads to accept the validity of a hierarchy of posts, since they have not usually been involved in their creation. Nor do teachers see them as having been created to assist them in the discharge of the essential task of the school, namely to facilitate the teaching and learning processes. The young probationary teacher in the first case study states that many teachers earn more, but teach less than he does, and he does not know why (p.25). The head of department who disrupts the lesson in the case study 'Interruptions' clearly sees the entry form for examinations as a higher priority than the lesson that is interrupted. Neither the teacher nor the class see it that way (p.75). Too often middle management has been seen as the distribution of the Head's patronage, a stepping-stone to senior posts, a device for buying loyalty, reward for the time-server and the sycophant,or a sinecure that has permitted the acquisition of a favoured teaching commitment or simply less teaching. The widespread concern of teachers that success in the classroom leads to promotion out of the classroom cannot simply be dismissed as sour grapes; middle management is often the recipient of significant concessions in return for lightening the Head's load, rather than improving the lot of the class teacher. It is our contention that such a view of middle management is reliant on the dispersal of power and authority by the Head, which may be more apparent than real. Since Heads can create posts and then proceed to do some or all of the job themselves, this is likely to produce strains on the post-holder, and to encourage others to regard them with resentment, envy, and even alienation. Staff not given middle management roles can resent being asked to undertake duties which they feel others are being paid to perform. They are deterred from taking action when they perceive that something should be done, because they lack the explicit authority to do it themselves. Meanwhile, lacking clear understanding of the nature of their role, heads of department, faculty, house or year may create work to justify their position, taking on what it would be better to share out, and taking care to please senior staff rather than serving their teaching colleagues. In the case study entitled 'Sharing', the head of department seizes the opportunity to involve teachers in preparing teaching materials. Without his initiative it would not have happened (p.73).

Middle management to serve the class teacher

Such an analysis does not mean, however, that there is no validity in middle management when viewed from the perspective of the class teacher's desk, but rather that such roles would require a different interpretation if they relied for their authority and validity on the extent to which they served the needs of the class teacher. Teachers have needs that cannot easily be satisfied either by their own efforts or by the efforts of colleagues with similar experience or status to themselves, and these needs can provide a more sure basis for the middle manager than the role derived solely from senior management. There are, after all, few teachers who would deny that they see the need, from time to time, to seek the guidance of fellow professionals who have the time, and perception, to respond to their needs. Such staff acquire a valid role, irrespective of any designated by the Head. These needs may be summarised as coordinating, counselling, involving, facilitating, evaluating, informing, supporting and resourcing the teacher. Although the teaching and learning processes occur, in the main, in separate classrooms, with distinct groups of students, there are numerous occasions where uncoordinated activities would hinder progress; for example, where resources do not allow for the simultaneous teaching of particular topics, a programme for the use of apparatus or of textbooks needs to be devised, and the same is true with the use of particular accommodation or of visual aids. Examination and assessment procedures require coordination, and the movement of pupils between teaching groups needs monitoring. Preparing work and teaching materials is very time consuming and rationalising these activities reduces the pressures on individual teachers. In the case study referred to above, the teacher who has volunteered to revise teaching material is immensely relieved when the head of department involves other members of the department in the same task (p.74). Tutor groups may benefit from the coordination of fund-raising activities for charity, and a system for conducting assemblies avoids last-minute panic. What is interesting about these examples, and there are many others that could be cited,is that such coordination is rarely very demanding; it can easily be done by even a junior member of staff, unless there is contention about 'fairness' and efficiency, or where there is a need to change existing practice. Then, arbitration is called for between competing factions and those whose enhanced status has been earned can exercise judgements. Here, the middle management role of coordinator is not essentially an administrative one, but is rather that of anticipating, avoiding or defusing conflict between close colleagues.

Teaching is an emotionally and intellectually demanding activity and requires a high level of professional skills if the confidence of students, parents and fellow professionals is to be won and maintained. In addition, colleagues bring into school many extraneous experiences that have a bearing on their conduct as teachers. It is also a job that is very difficult to perform adequately when the teacher is unwell. There can be few teachers who have not felt grateful to an accessible, approachable, knowledgeable and sympathetic colleague, with enough authority to do something, even if it is simply to listen, or take a class until composure is recovered. Teachers will search out someone near that they trust to perform this role; it is likely to be a middle manager. The head of year in the case study entitled 'Helping' plays a valuable counselling role to the teacher as well as to the girl in question (p.82).

Not all teachers are adept at getting involved in activities, both within the classroom and outside it. They may be shy, uncertain of their own capabilities, anxious not to offend those already involved, unsure of what is expected, and diffident about the appropriateness of certain initiatives. More senior colleagues can provide the spur to getting involved and advise about the way to do so. They can secure the invitation that encourages people to have a go.

Where there exists the notion of wanting to do things, and the willingness to undertake the work required, it does not always follow that things get done. To enable things to get underway, it may be necessary to create time, secure finance, gain authority, seek permission or obtain accommodation and these pre-conditions may be more easily met by a middle manager whose status gives him or her credibility as a facilitator.

While it is true that we all have some idea of how well we are doing our jobs, it is also true that evaluating worth, identifying our shortcomings and assessing our performance as teachers needs an external perspective. If this perspective is too remote from our daily routine as teachers, it will lack conviction, so our close but experienced and perceptive colleagues can be of great assistance in evaluating our actions and so help remove or minimise our faults, and more importantly, praise our strengths. The teacher in the case study entitled 'Developing' who is about to face an interview with the head of department is understandingly anxious, but finds the experience valuable because the middle manager in question knows her well, is familiar with her work and clearly has her interests at heart (p.80).

It is impossible for everyone to know everything about a school and the context in which it operates, yet staff are continually handicapped by not knowing even essential pieces of information. While the existence of effective middle management does not guarantee an information flow, it can and should make a major contribution to it. Middle managers can receive data quickly, disseminate it to those who need to know, and likewise, can collect facts and opinions from a relatively small group to pass on to others who need to know. Staff have a great deal to gain from having someone near who knows. This is especially true of staff who are new to an institution, whether or not they are new to teaching, for no brochure or handbook has yet been written that anticipates every question, nor are senior management so readily available, or always knowledgeable enough, to be able to help. They may, indeed, be somewhat remote and even aloof by the very nature of their tasks. The frank and open discussion of teaching groups and teaching spaces for the forthcoming school year which takes place in the case study 'Meeting (1)' is an example of keeping teachers informed and involving them closely in matters concerning their teaching programme. This is their major preoccupation. If information had simply been handed down from on high without explanation, there would have been a risk of frustrating some teachers and alienating others (p.77).

Even those staff who prefer to work on their own, and like the personal glory when what they do is successful, rarely shun a degree of help and support from others. That support may be an encouraging word, or an attentive ear, or may extend to practical assistance. Very often, to do things in school requires a team effort and clear and commited support from senior colleagues is the factor that, more than any other, ensures success.

One may see the middle manager, therefore, as a vital resource, without which the class teacher, of whatever level, would find the job more difficult. From ensuring that there are work schemes, or social events, to providing stocks of file paper or up-to-date information about a particular student, the head of department, faculty, house or year can, by organisation, example and personality, induct and develop colleagues by responding to their perceived needs.

The middle manager as initiator and leader of a team

It is not, however, sufficient to assert that the rationale for middle management relies on the fact that colleagues can recognise what they want, and expect them to provide it. Such managers are not merely reactive, responding to the whims and wishes of their department, faculty, house or year. There are situations in which junior teachers, and senior ones too, will benefit from middle managers taking the initiative, providing drive and energy, seeking to motivate, inspire and transform, even when there has been no apparent demand. The head of year in the case study entitled 'Meeting (2)' listens to the dissatisfactions voiced in the pub, accepts some of the blame and then takes a positive initiative to do something about the problems. He will put something on paper. He will suggest a programme of action. The issues will be fully discussed at a meeting of year tutors 'this week'. Middle managers themselves have needs and ambitions, as well as experience; that they see themselves as initiators, using their status and authority to achieve change is not to be construed as the usurping of a role, or to lack validity simply because junior colleagues do not at first approve. What is worth asking is whether the action will directly aid the teaching and learning function, or whether it seeks to impress the Head, to make life more difficult for subordinates, to extend power and influence, to aid promotion or other alternative aims. It is when middle managers see themselves as doing the Head's job that they run the risk of appearing either irrelevant or interfering. There are those who seem to collect tasks like others collect stamps and who act out a daily performance of problem-solving that serves largely to diminish their colleagues' authority. To justify their salary, they try to take over rather than share problems, feeling the constant pressure to prove that they are fit to be in charge by taking on all the tasks that there are around. These are middle managers who seek their own job satisfaction, not through the achievements of children, nor through the development of professional competence of staff, but by building their own image in the school.

If the management function of getting things done by, through and with others is to operate effectively in the professional climate of a staff, it can be seen to have a vital service and support element. It is

worth asking how many staff one person can support, rather than
how many one person can control. It is regrettable that the notion of
service and support is not more widely accepted or highly regarded in
this aspect of school life. Many essential service functions such as
resources production or careers work are of relatively low status,
though such activities are clearly designed to be a direct benefit to
staff and students. Often those who deal with tasks that aid the senior
management – for example, staff deputed to maintain the
administration of the examination system, staff duties, or timetable
construction – enjoy high status with time, space, extra salary and
even a telephone, office and secretarial help. Yet these tasks, in
execution if not in planning, really need little or no special knowledge
or experience, and could be understood and carried out by other than
teachers, once the ground rules had been established.

Summary

Our contention is, then, that there can be a clear rationale for middle
management when viewed from the classroom, and it is one that
recognises that there are necessary services to be performed on behalf
of class teachers and their students. If they assume a job specification
drawn up with the concept of supporting classroom activity rather
than sharing the Head's job, staff who perform these roles can enjoy a
very satisfying position in the school. To do the job well, such staff
would need to ask first what service they perform for the area of their
responsibility. They would need to begin by having respect for those
whom they support and perhaps by even liking them. They would
need to avoid having favourites or being patronising. They would
need to praise, persuade, correct, cajole, enable and involve. As fellow
teachers are even less likely to respond well to a directive than are
children, there is the need to influence and advise rather than
admonish and instruct. Above all, middle management, to be valued
and trusted, needs to take pleasure in the growing professionalism of
their team, for all benefit from a system that is mutually supportive.
There are those who carry the title of head of department and yet are
the sole teacher of that discipline in the school. This is not the sense of
the term as we are using it here. Such people manage themselves, and
the subject, and the students, but not a group of other staff. It is the
latter condition that characterises middle management and makes it
such a key element in any school. Effective teams of teachers provide

the generators for the power supply of a school and these teams demand leadership if they are to flourish. Departments or year groups that offer experience of team leadership to all as soon as they are showing signs that they are ready are likely to be vital, exhilarating teams to teach in; the people in such teams are likely to be more confident as teachers and the climate is likely to be a more favourable one for education to take place effectively.

Suggestions for further reading

BEST, R. *et al* (1980) *Perspectives on Pastoral Care* (London, Heinemann Educational Books).
BLACKBURN, K. (1975) *The Tutor* (London, Heinemann Educational).
MARLAND, M. (1974) *Pastoral Care* (London, Heinemann Educational).
MARLAND, M. (1971) *Head of Department* (London Heinemann Educational).
MARLAND, M. and HILL, S. (1982) *Departmental Management* (Heinemann Educational).

1. Principle: a Deputy Head negotiates a curriculum change

You are the Deputy Head with particular responsibility for the curriculum, and chair the curriculum committee which is representative of all faculties in the school. This committee is responsible for putting proposals for curriculum change to the senior management for approval and implementation. Recently, there has been a positive move from senior management to promote a course in Personal and Social Education beyond the third year into years IV and V. You have placed it on the agenda for the next meeting of your committee and are wondering what sort of reception the item will get. While the popularity of the subject has grown in years I to III there is considerable opposition to the idea that it should take up valuable time in the two years when examination subjects should have top priority. It is going to prove difficult to persuade individual members of your committee to give up faculty time to a subject which is not examined and has yet to gain real status in the school. It is taught by team-teaching methods within each year and the year heads are responsible for the course construction which is in a modular form. The coordination is very loose and has been carried out by your colleague the Deputy Head (Pastoral). Before the meeting of your curriculum committee takes place there is the usual meeting of the senior management team which takes place weekly. At that meeting you share with your colleagues your apprehensions about the anticipated difficulties when the curriculum committee debate the proposed extension of the Personal and Social Education course. Discussion at the meeting of the senior management team focuses on the role of the senior management in this situation. It could, of course, hand down an edict, which the faculties would have to accept, but this would lead inevitably to much resentment and to alienation. Such a process would be highly unpopular. What alternative strategies are there which do not involve an imposed solution? A lengthy debate might be embarked upon, aimed at persuading some faculty or faculties to surrender time in the week to the new course. This is a possible course of action but one which is likely to be very exhausting and very frustrating. Each faculty will go on the defensive and defend its corner with mounting reluctance to give up time in the timetable. True, one or two faculties may be prepared to concede the idea in principle, but when it comes to the amount of time to be given up further acrimony will take place. It is the Deputy Head (Administration), a pragmatic character who comes up with a further possibility. Unless you rely on 'consensus by exhaustion', there is no likelihood of any solution following the latter strategy. He asks what your committee is likely to agree on in the field of Personal and Social Education and after a pause receives the answer that everyone will eventually agree that it is a 'good thing', like justice or not beating your wife! So, he continues, why not let the committee discuss that, i.e. the educational value of the course to a child, perhaps to their child. Tell the committee at the outset that the implementation of it is not their problem. They merely have to decide whether or not the course goes into the curriculum of all children in years IV and V. If they agree in principle, or reach a consensus, then it will be the job of the senior management team to put it into practice in the timetable. People will, in the main, support decisions in which they have shared; the important strategy lies in framing the question so that it is one to which all may feel committed in principle. It will beimpossible for all to feel satisfied with the way it is put in practice. The decisions of the senior management team as arbitrator or mediator will not always be popular, but that is part of their function; that is the service which they perform for the staff who represent the faculties on your committee. They have a responsibility to carry out an executive function and because they carry it out jointly with other colleagues there is a greater possibility that their decisions will be accepted. The executive function discharged by an individual will much more readily be criticised as the exercise of prejudice or bias. Your joint prejudices will be much more widely tolerated. You are grateful to your colleagues for this jointly produced solution and proceed to modify the wording of your agenda accordingly.

2. Reputation: criticism of public examination results is voiced in a PTA committee meeting

The P.T.A. Committee had moved smoothly through its agenda and had listened approvingly to the detailed arrangements for the Christmas Fair from the Chairman. There would be a number of additional stalls and sideshows this year and she was hopeful that a considerable sum would be raised in response to the school's appeal for help with buying new textbooks. Some provisional arrangements for the proposed Spring Draw were also settled and soon it was time to consider any other business. At this point, a member of the committee who usually said little made a rather hesitant intervention. She wanted to refer to the recent publication of the school's examination results for last summer and first asked whether this was the proper place to bring it up. There was an embarrassed silence before the Chairman, having looked to the Head for support, asked the questioner if she would like to elaborate. She added, somewhat diffidently, that she and a number of other parents whom she frequently met at coffee-mornings were concerned about the results in History and Biology. This was attributed by her own son and by some of his friends to weak teaching and to difficulties in doing homework when textbooks had to be shared. She wondered what was being done to improve the situation in the current school year. There were murmurs of agreement from other members of the committee and the Chairman again looked to the Head for a response. The members of staff present, who included two of the deputies and one teacher of Biology but no teacher of History, also looked to the Head. The Head at first appeared a little taken aback, but nevertheless responded. She first regretted that this important matter had not been raised before the meeting, but hastened to add that she would rather it be raised at the school than be talked about outside in the neighbourhood. She offered to prepare a fuller reply to the question for the next meeting, but meanwhile would make one or two brief comments which might be helpful.

First, she indicated a number of items which had been bought recently with money raised by the parents, but stressed that resources still remained a serious problem in certain subjects. There had also been a number of problems over staffing in the departments concerned. The head of History had decided to take early retirement in the middle of last year and a pregnancy in the Biology department had not helped. She did not propose to comment on the quality of the teaching in either department, but would go so far as to say that the staffs of both departments had expressed their own concern already with the examination results. She saw the minutes of their regular meetings and was aware of this concern. She asked that parents who were concerned about the progress of individual children should make arrangements to see the year tutor concerned and if their anxieties remained to arrange an interview with her. This interim statement seemed to satisfy most parents present, although one parent who was also a governor of the school enquired whether these matters would be on the agenda of the next Governors' meeting. She was assured that the examination results would certainly be discussed at the meeting which would take place towards the end of the Autumn term.

In the pub after the meeting the Head and one of her Deputies were talking about the incident at the end of the meeting. The Head was anxious to get a reaction on how she had handled a tricky situation. The Deputy reassured her that she had coped very well, but wanted to know what would happen next. A commitment had been given to give a fuller response. Had this been wise? How much more was there to say? What was more important was how to avoid questions like this being asked in the future. The Head felt that questions of this nature might well be asked in the present climate and her concern was to devise a strategy to deal with them. Parents were entitled to a response and to an informed response. Therefore, she suggested that the matter be discussed at the meeting of senior management next Monday. Before the meeting, and to avoid insidious rumour, she would invite the head of Biology and the acting head of History to see her tomorrow for an up-to-date account of departmental discussions of the quality of teaching and to sound them out on their most serious resources problems. Above all, both felt that it was the responsibility of senior management to provide positive support for the departments concerned. Furthermore, they must not be seen to be isolated from their colleagues. Any strategy agreed by the senior management should be within an overall strategy of encouraging departments to review the quality of their teaching. This meant evaluation and the comments of both parents and pupils were forms of evaluation to be set beside other forms of evaluation undertaken by the teaching staff themselves.

While this issue was being discussed by the Head and her Deputy another parent joined them at their table. He offered them both a drink and then steered the conversation round to the behaviour of the children in bus queues.

3. Crisis: the day of a Deputy Head

You were appointed to the post of Deputy Head last September when
your school was reorganised as an 11–16 mixed comprehensive
school and lost its sixth form. As rolls fall the school will change from
eight forms of entry to six forms of entry. The Head of the former
11–18 High School applied unsuccessfully for the post of Principal of
one of the new sixth-form colleges and eventually was appointed to
the 11–16 school. He is becoming somewhat disillusioned and is
talking of early retirement. Meanwhile he spends considerable time
out of school on various committees, is a keen Rotarian and enjoys his
golf. You have replaced a Deputy who retired on reorganisation and
who was responsible for administration. Another Deputy, responsible
for Pastoral Care, is to take early retirement in the summer. She is
unlikely to be replaced. The remaining Deputy is responsible for the
curriculum and for the timetable. You seem to have inherited a 'mixed
bag' of responsibilities and, furthermore, the job specifications set out
in the staff handbook do not seem to correspond very closely with
what people actually do.

It is now February and you are assessing the rather indeterminate
nature of your job, while nevertheless finding plenty to do in meeting
crises as they occur.

One Friday morning you arrive a little later than usual and find
waiting outside your room a parent with a boy who has been away with
a serious illness. The Head's secretary hurriedly pushes a file onto
your desk and asks you to deal with it as the Head is about to take
Junior Assembly. She accompanies the file with a note of two more
staff absences to add to the two who are already off sick and to the
other two of whom you were told yesterday. You deal sympathetically
with the mother and her son and promise to arrange with the P.E. staff
for the boy to be excused games for a month. As they rise to go your
telephone rings. It is the Drama teacher who asks if she can have her
lessons covered for the last two periods that afternoon for an extra
rehearsal of the play which is to be presented soon after half-term.
You hesitate in view of the last minute nature of the request, but she is
insistent and you agree. You ask her to be sure to tell the children
concerned to get themselves excused from their classes. There is now
a long list of absentees for one reason or another. You rush off to the
staffroom to amend the list of stand-ins for the absentees on the
noticeboard. You are greeted by groans from some of the 'victims' and
by barbed comments from others about the absence rate: 'What

migraine again, it must be Friday!'. However, you have put yourself down for a substantial share of the day's extra lessons and have included both the other Deputies in the day's list.

You dash off to take one of these classes and soon find out that they have not been left any work to do. You improvise and peace descends once you have set some written work. As you sit in with this class, you think of all the jobs you had lined up for today because you normally are free of lessons on Friday. This had been timetabled deliberately because Friday is normally a busy day. You have been asked by the Head to work out some plans for fund-raising which might be put to the P.T.A. Committee on the following Monday evening. Then there is Jennie Thompson. She asked you yesterday if she could come to your room for a private chat about her future. Apparently, she is missing her sixth-form work. She added that she had never been able to talk freely to the Head. You had agreed to see her in a free period after break. Now that interview will have to be put off. On Friday afternoon it is usual for the senior management to get together to chat over the week's happenings. You would have to miss out that meeting too. As these various different jobs go through your mind you begin to wonder if it was wise to have put yourself down for so much teaching on that day. Where should your priorities be? Were you really paid the salary of a Deputy Head to take other people's classes? By the time the bell goes for break you have convinced yourself that you have been kind but foolish.

You return to the staffroom, explain to Jennie Thompson that you cannot see her today and have a word with the head of P.E. about the boy who is to be excused games. There is just time to grab a cup of coffee before you are off down the corridor to take another class. On your way you pass the music suite from which a very unmusical sound is emerging. It is Nigel Thorpe who is endeavouring to settle down a third-year class. Nigel is an amiable, willing and ineffectual colleague, aged 43, who has difficulty in maintaining discipline with some classes. He has a history of nervous trouble which began soon after he joined the staff some years ago as head of Music, Scale 2. You pause in the doorway for a few moments and, seeing you there, the class begins to settle down. You quickly extract two particularly vocal members of the class who have a reputation for causing trouble and take them with you to the class you are teaching. Nigel looks immensely relieved and resumes his seat at the piano.

At the end of the afternoon you eventually find your way to the closing stages of the senior management meeting. A discussion is taking place about routines and how they might be overhauled. You have one or two pertinent points to make about routines in the case of staff absence and you make them quite strongly:

1. Staff should let you know as early as possible before an absence, if they know they are going to be away.
2. Staff who are unable to let you know beforehand and are unavoidably absent through sickness should let the school know before 9.00 a.m. in the morning.
3. Staff who know that they are going to be away should leave work for all their classes with their head of department.

The Deputy Head who is retiring observes that all that information is stated in the staff handbook. You hastily respond that there is not much point in it being in the staff handbook if it doesn't happen. Your colleagues are rather taken aback by your sudden sharpness of tone and you apologise, muttering that it has been a rather heavy day. 'Your trouble is, you've been teaching too many classes today', says the Head with a benign smile. The other Deputy looks thoughtful and interjects to report a conversation in the staffroom at lunchtime. Apparently, a number of teachers who might have lost free periods but for your action had voiced their jocular appreciation of your readiness to take classes, one or two of which were difficult ones. The meeting moves on to consider how routines can be monitored and reinforced regularly to make sure that what is supposed to be happening is really happening. All recognise that it is certainly the job of senior management to see that routines are followed.

You share cars with a young teacher who lives not far from your home and on the way that evening are chatting over the events of the day. He expresses surprise that you have been teaching all day, and asks whether you don't have more important things to do. Deputy Heads always seem to be too busy to teach. Nevertheless, he thinks it's a good thing. 'Gives us the feeling that you are one of us, and you know what it's about. After all, schools are about teaching I suppose, really.'

You drop him outside his house and reflect as you drive on to begin the weekend that perhaps it wasn't such a bad idea to take those classes and share with colleagues in the essential activity which binds teachers together on a staff and for which schools exist. It might help your credibility as a new Deputy Head too.

4. Development: a Head counsels a senior colleague who is seeking promotion

Len Fuller is head of P.E. and is aged 34. He was appointed to your school five years ago after experience in a small mixed grammar school. He has adapted himself well to the wider requirements of your seven-form entry mixed comprehensive school.

He holds a Scale 4 post now and is thinking about his next move. He has talked to you about his ambitions to become a Deputy and then a Head and you have encouraged him to begin to submit applications for posts of Deputy Head. You are rather surprised to receive a flurry of requests for references for a variety of posts: two are for senior teacher posts and one is for an adviser's post in a neighbouring authority.

In preparing your replies you note his strong points:
(a) He is an effective teacher of P.E. and his discipline is good.
(b) He is a good organiser of sporting events and also of your Annual Summer Fair.
(c) He is a graduate Chemical Engineer and has a Diploma from Loughborough College.
(d) His sporting specialisms were swimming and rugby. He has acquired coaching and refereeing qualifications in athletics, basketball, volleyball and trampolining.
(e) He is a good team leader and motivates the members of his department.
(f) His personal file reveals that he has attended a number of courses over recent years and assisted the authority's inspectors in a successful in-service course last year.
(g) He has given the school a local reputation for achievement in games.

Yesterday, Len was unsuccessful in his first interview for a senior teacher post. He comes to tell you about the interview. He confesses that he was very unprepared for the interview and didn't do himself justice. He now seeks your advice on a number of issues.

First, he wonders if he is too old for promotion. Should he first become a senior teacher before applying for a job as a Deputy Head? Should he seek secondment and some further qualification? He is self-conscious of his specialism in P.E. Should he seek classroom teaching of a subject other than P.E? What opportunities for further promotion or experience are likely to be available in this school without moving?

You ask him to see you in a day or so, when you have had time to think about his position and merely observe that you had not thought his desire for promotion was urgent. He replies that the recently completed Sports Centre was giving him a great deal of personal satisfaction and he does find his present job very rewarding. However, he feels that he owes it to himself to seek promotion before the opportunity goes. He adds, as he leaves your room, that his wife is exerting considerable pressure on him to seek advancement in his career before it is too late.

You are left pondering what your considered advice should be when Len returns in a few days' time. You wonder whether you have perhaps been realistic in giving him general encouragement to seek promotion, without assessing his situation more clearly. Len and many other teachers like him face considerable problems in developing their professional careers in the present and future climate of schools. Opportunities for promotion are not going to be nearly so numerous as they have been in the past. The education service is contracting and there is no doubt that many teachers who, in the past, entertained aspirations to become Deputy Heads or Heads will not, in the future, attain these positions. This fact has significant implications for senior management. In the past senior managers and Heads in particular have given support both in the form of personal advice and in the form of written references to those members of their teaching staffs who were applying for promotion. In the present and future circumstances what form is that support going to take?

Len Fuller is a first-rate classroom teacher. He manages the team in his department well. He is engaged in a multitude of out-of-school activities. In other words, he is already a highly successful professional, but bearing in mind his particular main subject and the state of the market his promotion prospects are not good. Equally, you cannot evade your responsibility to provide Len with counselling about his professional development, difficult though it may be to formulate this advice. You need to be supportive, but at the same time you must be realistic. You begin to tease out some positive alternatives: a switch of emphasis to Science teaching or a course in management, perhaps leading to the job as warden of a Sports Centre or a Leisure Centre, are two possibilities. At the same time you will need to counteract any naïve optimism by conveying a clear picture of the difficulties of the present and of the future. Any targets which you set will need to be realistic and attainable. You will be expected to show some vision; you will also be wise to express your appreciation and even congratulate him on his present performance.

You begin to realise how different and how much more complex is the task of senior management nowadays in counselling staff about their future careers. The exhortations of the past are no longer appropriate and you need to ask yourself what frame of mind you want Len to go away in after his next interview with you. Above all, he must not be fobbed off with platitudes, bland assertions or promises which cannot be fulfilled. You will hope to maintain or even to lift his confidence and at the same time portray a realistic picture of the present and of the future.

As you begin to think through the positive support which it is your responsibility to give to Len Fuller, your own confidence may falter. You do not look forward to the interview, but it must be faced because many other such interviews will follow, some much more difficult than this one.

5. Arbitration: conflict between two teachers

It seemed a most unreasonable request to Frank Knowles. Frank was a conscientious and meticulous teacher of Geography whose room was always a model of tidiness and order. Everything was in its place: textbooks aligned in the cupboards, maps put away in the chests, lively examples of childrens' work on the walls. He prided himself on his audio-visual aids and had a splendid collection of slides put together with painstaking care from many visits and excursions. The overhead projector was always at the ready and indexed boxes of transparencies provided his classes with diagrams and notes. The one thing Frank could not abide was having to teach in any other room but his own and now he had been approached from that new young historian to ask if he would be prepared to swap rooms on alternative Fridays in order that she could have a room with a black-out. It really did seem most unreasonable to Frank for all sorts of reasons. First, because it had never happened before. The members of the History department had always been happy to teach all over the school. They had never had a suite of rooms and Frank suspected that it was a report from a visiting H.M.I. which had prompted the awkward rearrangement for putting all the so-called 'humanities' departments together in one block of buildings. Frank was also rather horrified at the thought of the particular form which she proposed to bring into his room, while he took his ten 'A' level candidates down the corridor to her room.

Putting it as politely as he could, Frank explained that it wasn't really very practicable. He was sorry, of course, not to be more helpful.

He thought that would be the end of the matter, until a couple of days later he was approached by his head of department, Felicity Brown. Felicity had taken up her appointment last term and had already proposed one or two other changes which had upset Frank, like changing his old and tried textbook for Form 2 for a lot of worksheets. She now sought his cooperation, as she put it, in 'helping these young teachers to find their feet'. Couldn't he see his way to leave his room every alternative week to let Jenny, as she called her, make use of a set of slides on 'Transport through the ages'. It seemed such a pity, as she had apparently gone to a lot of trouble to borrow them from the Teachers' Centre.

Frank was unyielding. If the History department was going in for this sort of thing then they must get some rooms blacked-out. Well yes, countered Felicity, that was all part of the long-term plan for the Humanities block but, of course, with the cuts it was all delayed and meanwhile couldn't Frank be accommodating? No, he was sorry but this was the thin end of the wedge. If he gave in to this request, it would be the first of many. No, he was very sorry, but it wasn't on.

Felicity went away from this interview rather thoughtful. She was not anxious to reveal to Alan Frobisher, the head of the History department that she had not been able to handle Frank. She did nothing for a few days.

On Friday afternoon Felicity was well into her lesson with 5A, when there was a knock on the door. It was Frank and clearly he was beside himself. Could he see her for a moment on an urgent matter. He had arrived to take his sixth-form group and found his room occupied by 'young Jenny' and a far from orderly fourth form. The black-out blinds were drawn, the slide projector was purring and all he could see in the darkness was a splendid picture of a sedan chair. Frank was very cross and what did she propose to do about it? Lamely, Felicity agreed that there must be some misunderstanding. She promised to see Alan Frobisher at an early opportunity. Frank swept off, his 'A' level textbook and a batch of essays to return under one arm.

Felicity's meeting with Alan after school that day was disconcerting. Yes, there was a misunderstanding. Alan was under the impression that she had agreed to arrange for the exchange to take place. In fact, she had been most helpful and he had told Jenny that there was no problem and she could go ahead and use the room that week on Friday. Wasn't this perhaps rather a lot of fuss about nothing? After all they knew what Frank was like, an 'old woman' where his precious room was concerned. It would do him good to be shaken up a bit, sometimes. Perhaps she should have another chat with Frank. Besides, it was rather awkward to have to go back on what he had told Jenny. He would feel rather a fool. He was sure Frank would be reasonable.

At the golf club on Saturday morning, Frank ran into Joe Railton who was one of the Deputy Heads and an old friend. He stopped briefly to recount to Joe his embarrassment of Friday afternoon. Surely Joe could sort it out. A word in the ear of Felicity would put her right. Joe wasn't so sure, but said he would think about it and went off to the first tee.

On Monday morning after the school had settled down, Joe went looking for his colleague Deputy Head, Barry Ferris, and shared the problem with him. Barry and Joe usually met like this, quite informally, fairly early in the week to consider any current problems. This was a ticklish one. At what level should it be dealt with? Clearly both heads of departments were already involved, but what about Frank and Jenny? How urgent was it. In terms of the timetable, of course, they had until a week on Friday, but in terms of mending the rift in personal relationships the matter was perhaps more pressing. Should it be left to the two heads of department to sort out? After all, it seemed a low-level business really.

After a discussion they decided first that there was certainly no need to involve the Head. On the other hand, there was a case for senior management to become involved as arbitration seemed necessary. Barry thought he was the one to deal with it as he had responsibility for curricular matters and it involved two academic departments. Joe's involvement need not be divulged.

Barry saw both heads of department that day after school and the meeting took place quite amicably. Felicity was particularly relieved to have Barry's support and when Alan had left the room confessed: 'I'm glad you intervened, Barry, when you did. I was in a bit of a spot and was going to bring up the whole black-out business again at the next head of department meeting in a fortnight. That wouldn't have helped much would it!' Barry smiled and said, 'Well, when you see Frank, you can blame it all on me.'

After she had left, he made a note for his next meeting with the Head. It read: 1.   Black-out; humanities. 2   middle managers; staff development?

6. Fracas: disruption in a class

When Ann Lomax looked at the staffroom noticeboard and saw that she was substituting for a colleague in the Art department she swore quietly under her breath. Friday was the deadline for her examination papers to be prepared and into the office for duplication. She hadn't even started to prepare them yet. She also noted that the Art room was not available because it was full of scenery and properties for the play which was to be presented in a fortnight's time. The Art teacher in question was hectically busy with a select group of young artists completing what it had not been possible to finish off in out-of-school time. Ann was a teacher of Mathematics and had no intention of improvising an art lesson in an ordinary classroom. She grabbed a Mathematics textbook with lots of examples and a handful of exercise paper and set off down the corridor in search of the fourth-year art set which had been displaced into room 23.

The class was already in her room when she arrived. They were a smallish group, mostly girls and were standing round chatting. Ann entered the room briskly and gave a peremptory instruction to them to sit down. Some turned round and looked at her, recognising a young teacher who had joined the school last September. Only a few of this group had ever met her in a classroom before. She produced her neat stack of paper, put it down on a desk in front of the class and instructed the girl sitting on that desk to give out the pieces of paper. Then she turned round and started to write some mathematics examples on the blackboard. 'Why can't we have art, miss?' She turned to answer the questioner and realised that only a small number of the class had settled in their desks. 'Because I'm a teacher of maths and this is a maths lesson. Besides, the art room is out of use'. There was a murmur of disapproval and a harsher statement from the former questioner: 'I don't want to do sums, miss'. Ann focused on the girl in question, who was standing in the centre aisle. She did not recognise her, but ordered her sharply to sit down. The girl did not move and a quiet fell on the room. 'What's your name?' snapped Ann Lomax. 'Tracy Arnold, miss', replied the girl, and added quickly, 'I don't see why we have to do sums miss, when we've got art. I hate sums anyway.' Ann Lomax moved towards the girl who had now gone red in the face. She made as if to put her into her seat, but as she raised her arm Tracy knocked it away and shouted, 'Don't you touch me, you cow!' Ann went white, stopped, turned round and ran out of the room for help. She found help in the person of the second Deputy Head, Eddie

Fallon, who had a room in that building. Eddie listened to Ann's gabbled version of the incident, as they returned to room 23. Tracy had disappeared and, on enquiry from the rest of the class, it appeared likely that she had fled to the girls' toilets. Eddie told Ann to stay with the class and went in pursuit of Tracy. On his way he picked up one of his 'old hands', Barbara Downing, whom he briefed quickly. She found Tracy quietly sobbing in the toilets and persuaded her somewhat reluctantly to accompany her to Eddie's room. Both Eddie and Barbara knew Tracy and her family from many earlier encounters. In fact, there was a long history of defiance and aggressive behaviour, but she had not raised her hand to a teacher.

Eddie spoke quietly, but firmly, to Tracy who sat sullen and morose looking at the floor. He did not start by asking a lot of questions, but simply explained that what she had done was serious and that she would have to be suspended from school until the matter was sorted out. The Head was out at a meeting, but he was able to suspend her himself, and proposed to ask Miss Downing to take her home in her car. Her parents would be written to and invited to come in and talk to the Head in a few days' time. Tracy listened without saying anything and then suddenly blurted out, 'But she shouldn't have hit me, should she? I only asked her why we couldn't do art.' Eddie didn't say any more. Barbara took her home. She had a house-key fortunately, and was quite used to letting herself in.

Eddie next arranged to see Ann after break. He found someone to take her class and sat her down, clutching a cup of coffee and still shaken. He asked her quietly to tell him what had happened, and this she did haltingly, slightly confused about the sequence of events. Eddie let her talk and describe what had happened in her own way. He took some notes unobtrusively, quoting where possible Ann's own words. He explained the routines about suspension to her. She had only a vague notion of what happened in such cases although it was all set out formally in the staff handbook. It all seemed very different when it actually happened. Gradually, she began to regain her composure and to express her anxieties and uncertainties about her own behaviour. It had all happened so suddenly. What should she have done? Had anything like this happened before? What would the Head say? Eddie didn't attempt to answer all these questions. He listened and listened and as Ann went quieter said, 'Well, I don't know about you but I could do with a drink. Shall I see what I've got in that cupboard?'

7. Climate: restoring a school atmosphere which is deteriorating

It is about 3 p.m. on a Friday afternoon in February when you arrive back at school from your meeting at County Hall. It has rained most of the day. As you park your car, you cast a baleful eye round the playground. Wet litter looks so much more dreary than dry litter. There are very few children about in the playground and as you enter the building the noise and movement seems somehow worse than usual, even for a wet breaktime. A large boy comes rushing down the staircase and is halted by the strident shout of a teacher on duty. A group of excited girls disappear round a corner arm-in-arm. There are several isolated shrieks, followed by a gust of laughter, then a teacher's sharp high-pitched reproof. You are aware of noise, disturbance and the smell of warm, wet clothing as you make your way hurriedly to your room.

There is the usual pile of papers and letters awaiting you on your desk and you have scarcely set down your briefcase and removed your raincoat before your secretary is in the room armed with her notepad. 'I'm glad you're back early. There's an urgent message from the Head of St Monica's. Will you ring her back. I think it's about the fence again – and the Farrell family have been on the 'phone again this morning – dad this time. He insists on seeing you about Jeremy and is not happy seeing his year tutor.'

There is a knock on the door and Arthur Smith, the second Deputy puts his head round. 'Ah, I thought I saw your car. Can I have a word at 4 o'clock? Won't keep you, but it's the bus company again. Some damage to seats this time, I gather.' He disappears.

You sit down and wonder what to tackle first, deciding that it had better be Miss Royce of the girls' school. Their playing fields adjoin yours. However, before you can gather your thoughts, the 'phone rings. It's the head of lower school and she asks if the matter of decorations, particularly of the girls' toilets can be put on the agenda for the senior management meeting on Monday after school. Scarcely have you put down the 'phone when there is another knock on the door. This time it is the first Deputy, who has a regular appointment on Friday afternoon when he is free. You relax, sit back in your chair. You are pleased to see him and smile, a trifle sardonically. 'Come in and sit down, Jim. You are just the man. You can tell me why the place seems to be going to pieces today.'

He slumps onto a chair and grins back. 'Well, funny you should mention it, but I was about to report that today everything is a shambles. Of course, there's been a lot of staff absence and some rather feeble excuses too. I suppose it's the time of the year for people to feel under the weather. They usually let us know in good time if they are sick and most of them set work for their classes. It's not always happening, I'm afraid.' You buzz your secretary for some tea and continue your chat. It hasn't been like this for some time. You have a good teaching staff and have always prided yourself on the atmosphere of the school. The Autumn term went well, little absence and no serious problems of discipline. There was a very good production of *Guys and Dolls* before Christmas.

You are still discussing the state of the school when Arthur Smith joins you at the end of the school day to toss his problems with the bus company into the pool of your anxieties. 'Just listen to that row in the corridors. We'd better sort it out before we settle down to anything else.'

The three of you leave the Head's room and add your weight to that of the staff on duty. Soon a weekend calm begins to descend on the school building and cleaners are scurrying about. You return to your former discussion. 'Well, whatever else there is on the agenda, we'd better have a look at the state of the place, on Monday evening'. You ask the others what they think. 'Yes, I agree', replies Arthur, 'We certainly need to tackle it together, all seven of us, like we did the last time, otherwise it will get on top of us and we are not having that.'

There's a mutter of approval from Jim who adds, 'Yes, it's the general climate, isn't it? That includes everything; punctuality to classes, absenteeism among staff and pupils, how the staff talk to the kids, all that stuff.' You agree. 'And then there's litter, graffiti, movement about the building and behaviour on buses. It's all of a piece, isn't it?'

You decide to give this matter priority on the agenda for Monday's meeting and sum it up thus: 'If the senior management doesn't tackle this sort of thing, then nobody will. They will all bitch about it in the staffroom and that's understandable. You can't expect a teacher in a classroom to see the whole picture. That's our job.'

The three of you part for the weekend and an hour later, after working through some of your papers, you pack some others into your briefcase and finally make one or two notes on your pad. In the corridor you bump into the caretaker. He has a rueful expression. 'Can't think what gets into them in wet weather. Some of my cleaners have been giving me a bad time about the hall floor. Good job I've got a broad back.' You smile in response. 'Yes, George, and by the way, come and see me first thing on Monday morning. I'd like your advice on one or two things.'

As you leave the building and climb into your car you reflect with some relief on the support you receive from the senior management team. Without them, you would find the job more difficult, more stressful and more lonely. As a team, you seem to have built the sort of relationships which mean that crises like the present ones are shared. You are aware that some of the teaching staff think you delegate too many things to other people but you wouldn't be comfortable running the school any other way. Mind you, building up the right sort of relationships takes a long time. You have done a lot of listening in the process.

Questions for discussion

1. Given a hierarchial pay structure, can a school operate on any other basis than that of hierarchy?
2. Identify the issues over which senior management, or the Head alone, should have total discretion.
3. By what processes might a school arrive at the role definition of its senior management?
4. When major disagreements occur within a school, what strategies would you prefer to employ?
5. In any staff appraisal scheme, who appraises the Head?
6. What are the means by which staff gain access to the Head and Deputies? Are the links formal or informal? Should senior staff operate an 'open door' policy?
7. How can a Head reconcile the need to be involved fully in the life of the school, and yet play a part in the life of the local authority, the locality and the professional scene.
8. How is a teacher best prepared for a senior management role?
9. What responsibilities do senior managers have for new entrants to the profession and for teachers who have newly arrived at a school?
10. How can senior managers influence the 'climate' or ethos of a school?
11. What role(s) should be played by senior staff in the staff development programme of a school?
12. What can senior managers do about their own staff development?
13. Is it a good idea for the responsibilities of a senior management to be rotated over a period of time? If so, how is this to be arranged?
14. Is there a role for experienced heads or senior staff to act as consultants to other schools?

In-service project work

1. What do you think are the job specifications of the senior management in your school? Check these against the actual job specifications (if there are any) or with the individuals themselves.
2. Discuss a programme of management training for senior management, including a practical element.
3. Compose a series of letters, memoranda and other documents

which can be used in an in-tray exercise for senior management training.

4. Role play the meeting of the senior management team which takes place on the Monday evening following the incidents described in the case study entitled 'Climate'.

5. Make a reciprocal arrangement to spend a day with your opposite number in another secondary school and for your counterpart to spend a day with you.

6. Set up a series of interviews for an imaginary post in a secondary school. Provide a job specification. Role play the interviews, with members of the group acting as candidates for the post and as members of the interviewing panel. Using closed-circuit television, video-tape the interviews for later discussion.

7. Invite members of the group to outline their careers so far on paper. Then, in pairs, exchange these details and, acting as the Head in turn, engage in a dialogue each counselling the other about his or her future career.

Chapter 10

Senior Management

The development of a senior management team in secondary schools

Although the use of the term 'senior management' in a school context is a relatively recent development, the notion that there should be a Headteacher who has sole charge of the institution has been giving way to the view that a group of senior staff, the Head, Deputies and even senior teachers share between them the task of running the school for some time. Even in secondary schools, this change has not been accepted universally, but generally it is acknowledged by the whole staff that appointment to a senior position means joining the people 'in charge'. However, the traditional authority of the Head, although now increasingly constrained by outside pressures, remains powerfully evident within the profession, and is regularly reinforced by those outside the school. Parents, employers, local residents and visitors expect to contact the Head, because they wish to deal with the person responsible for the school. Governors see the Head in similar terms, and can point to the Articles of Government of most schools as proof of the Head's authority. The Inspectorate deals primarily with the Head, and Local Authorities' personnel, who welcome the clear-cut simplicity of the 'in-line' management model, like to deal with the Head and are often disconcerted at having to deal with anyone else, except a named Deputy in the Head's absence.

That a small group is able to assume roles originally performed by one individual is seen as sensible delegation by the Head to avoid being over burdened. Thus the growth of team management has depended on each individual Head's preferences and capacities. Others are brought into senior management by the patronage of the Head, assuming functions discarded by the person who alone has the power to pick and choose roles. The very term 'Deputy Head' implies that the holder has a role legitimised only in the Head's absence, i.e. when called upon to deputise. Traditionally then, and largely in current practice, British schools are organised around a single personality, the Head, who gathers around him or her a small group who share the pressures, advise and extend his or her presence. Such a system flourishes and is largely unchallenged by the rest of the profession. That is to say, while the decisions and actions of senior management groups are often challenged, their right to make decisions or to take particular actions is not.

If the collective perceptions of so many people inside and outside the profession are that schools are run by Heads aided by a small number of senior staff, is it not enough to define senior management simply as those staff entrusted by the Head to make decisions about the running of the school? Should not those more junior colleagues, class teachers and middle managers alike, defer to those set in authority over them, accepting the directives given to them and then carrying out these directives to the best of their ability? After all, they can, in doing so, hope that, in time, they can exchange their subordinate role for a senior post themselves one day.

That relatively few staff seriously question this view, and that most readily grant that senior colleagues have authority over them, does not mean that such authority is necessarily valid, nor does it mean that such views are appropriate. As we have already stated, the development of hierarchies in secondary schools took place progressively as the schools became larger institutions, and this is not a satisfactory form of organisation for a school. Handy, looking at schools from the standpoint of an industrial management specialist, sees the 'role culture' of bureaucratic hierarchies as inappropriate for school organisation and suggests the 'task culture' with its teams loosely linked into networks may be more suitable to a secondary school's needs:

> Interestingly, however, modern businesses are moving away from hierarchies to networks in response to the need for more flexibility and in order to give more room for the individual. It may be that in aping the bureaucracy of large businesses the secondary school has been adopting a theory of management that is already out of date. (p.16).

There is a high price to be paid for running schools on a hierarchical model, not least when it suits subordinate staff to disassociate themselves from the decisions of their superiors because those decisions are unwelcome ones. In addition, senior staff can often feel isolated from their colleagues, miss the immediate contact with students, and feel that they have moved, or have been moved, away from those very experiences that brought them into teaching in the first place and have given them satisfaction and reward, towards activities that alienate them from others. Too often, staff who gain a senior management position find that their pleasure on achieving promotion is replaced by dissatisfaction at being required to operate in situations for which they are unprepared.

An alternative approach: the supportive executive model

However, it is our contention that, as with middle management, there is an approach to senior management that sees such roles differently. This approach envisages closer, not more distant, involvement with colleagues; more, not less, involvement with students; and relies upon a stronger justification than tradition, or external expectations. If senior management sees its function as teachers, not merely administrators; as executives, not legislators; as coordinators, custodians of the public image, not dictators; as supporters, not judges; as facilitators, not restrainers; involvers, not excluders; then they may rely not on unreasoning, begrudging acceptance of their 'power' but may enjoy an enthusiastic partnership based upon their being seen by fellow teachers, more as a resource and less as a threat.

If one views senior management from the perspective of a newly qualified member of the teaching staff of a school, it is reasonable to ask what functions that member of staff needs to have performed by senior management to improve the quality of his or her teaching. It is also reasonable to establish a pre-condition to the effective partnership; that the senior managers demonstrate, in all that they do that they have the well-being and education of young people as their professional priority. When the major preoccupation of the teaching staff is teaching, those who betray that their enthusiasm for promotion is to escape from teaching cease to share the common professionalism which develops mutual respect and confidence. Indeed, the first and the most important function that senior colleagues can perform for the whole staff is the sharing of the experience of teaching. From their experience senior staff should be able to provide a wealth of knowledge and understanding about the teaching and learning activity that is readily available to all who seek it, or could benefit from it. To demonstrate how little teaching matters by shunning class contact, or by taking a notional place on the timetable,but regularly failing to turn up, or by never talking publicly about the delights and disasters of children's company is to lose professional contact with colleagues. This breeds disenchantment, cynicism, and even contempt. The common link between all staff in schools is children, and this extends beyond teachers to school nurses, librarians, secretaries, technicians, caretakers and cleaning staff. Senior management gain esteem when they identify with the students' well-being and do not substitute other, less worthy issues such as administrative procedures, problems about paperwork, window-dressing or matters of protocol.

The case study entitled 'Crisis' illustrates an important role of a Deputy Head in sharing the teaching load of colleagues by standing in for absentees. His younger colleague comments at the end of the day, 'It gives us a feeling that you are one of us and you know what it's about'. (p.103).

While in no way excluding the necessary contribution of contemporaries and of middle managers, it is valuable for a new arrival to the school to recognise that all senior staff have a responsibility for the induction of the newcomer, although one person may specialise in it. Confidence established in the first few impressionable days is likely to last, and such induction is less about structure and organisation, which can be achieved through the staff handbook, than about relationships, the climate and ethos which underpins attitudes to the 'clients' and the difficulties involved in securing a place in those relationships. The young entrant to the profession in our first case study would have appreciated the opportunity to share such problems with a senior member of staff and with junior colleagues, but the induction scheme did not work well. It was given insufficient priority by the Deputy Head concerned (p.24). The simple admission that the Head or Deputy not only has experienced, but is experiencing, the problem of maintaining motivation in a particular class, or takes time to think out a response to a difficulty of classroom management, reinforces the concept that all are teachers and there is value in developing the expertise of all.

Implicit in the tutorial role of senior management towards new, though not exclusively probationer, staff is the need to convey something of the school style. Each teacher is unique and the school will always be an amalgam of many different personalities interacting, but there is an extent to which there needs to be an element of 'coherence'. Attitudes to students and colleagues, as well as visitors, are created and defined to a degree by senior management, since their

approach will be imitated by others. The way in which children are
spoken to, the style of referring to colleagues, and the response to
those who wish to visit will directly affect the tone of the classroom.
The 'all-change' system of lessons in a secondary school means the
staff receive classes fresh from other teachers' methods and the
immediate experience of one teacher colours the children's response
to the next. Senior staff can explain the reasoning behind current
practice and advise on style when a teacher is making a major
departure from the norm for that school.

As well as the tone and style of addressing people there is clearly a
need to define, explain and monitor the effectiveness of 'whole
school' policies. That is not to argue that policy-making at school level
has to be the prerogative of senior management, for we see a vital role
for all the staff in this respect, but it is essential that the school has
coherent policies, and it is the senior management's function to
ensure that these exist, and are understood by all. Staff would not
welcome uncoordinated anarchy and the school must devise some
mechanism to ensure a smooth-running, widely understood system.
Thus it may not be that senior managements decide or make the laws,
but they are there to see that laws are made and, especially, that they
are carried out in the interests of effective learning of the individuals
involved. Staff like the assurance that what they are doing is not being
done alone, that efforts, for example, to improve the environment are
not piecemeal, or that duties are interpreted in a similar fashion by
each duty team. They have the right to expect that policy duly arrived
at is then put into practice, even though this may involve tackling
individuals about their shortcomings. School policy that is ignored is
not policy at all, and it is the executive function of the senior
management to see that it does exist. In the case study called 'Climate'
the Head and the two Deputy Heads determine together to take a
firm grip on a situation which is getting out of hand. They recognise
that class teachers cannot see the whole picture. If the senior
management does not tackle these problems of ethos and atmosphere
by establishing the norms then nobody will. (p.112).

In any lively school there is bound to be conflict. Laudable activities
developed by different faculties, departments, houses, years or class
teachers may cut across each other; resources are few and disputes
occur. There needs to be a judicial function in any society and the role
of arbitrator is inevitable; the question is, simply, who performs this
role and how? The case study 'Arbitration' illustrates the complexities
of this situation, particularly the need for senior management to bring

to bear skills in human relationships when dealing with contrasting personalities (p.106). Wise senior management may see that the need to maintain harmonious relationships requires different responses to different circumstances. There are occasions when what is needed is a conciliation service, bringing together the disputing parties, so that, with a third force present, they can resolve the differences themselves On other occasions,it may be necessary to get two sides in a dispute to agree the need for arbitration and to hand over the problem to an even-handed senior member or group of staff, with a willingness to abide by their decision. What is being sought by senior managers, is the coordination of the efforts of all staff, so that there is little or no friction in the daily routine of the school. Conflicts can be resolved, or at least apparently resolved, by dictat; rarely do the aggrieved parties do anything but resent such a solution. Most staff, however, would see and respect the need for adjudication where talking out a problem with the interested parties had failed to provide an answer.

Just as staff will use senior management when they are in conflict with fellow staff to help them resolve disputes, so they see the value of such colleagues when they want something done and lack the resources or influence to bring it about themselves. Teachers and non-teachers with ideas about improving the learning environment, whether it be the physical conditions, course content or methodology, generally find that resources in the form of space, time, staff, equipment or money are required and senior management, if it is going to promote a vigorous and exciting school, must be ready to make things happen. The negotiations about introducing new material into the curriculum of years 4 and 5 which feature in the case study entitled 'Principle' illustrate how the Deputy Head in question endeavours to seek a positive outcome to what appears a most uncompromising clash of interests. Such a function as a facilitator contrasts sharply with the negative role frequently adopted by senior staff in which they find even more plausible reasons why initiatives should not be encouraged. To the junior or middle manager, the restrainer's role is an irksome one, much resented. It may, of course, be necessary. Resources may simply neither exist, nor be in the capacity of the school to provide. What is proposed may be in conflict with the school's declared policy or find disfavour with the Governors, the L.E.A. or parents, but much that would be welcomed relies heavily on senior staff if not to be thwarted at the outset. It is also true that failure to secure the resources for innovation or improvement has a cumulative impact, and leads to disillusion, just as a successful enterprise greatly encourages others.

The role of senior management in staff development

Professional people working in schools recognise an obligation to the young people they teach to develop their competence. Few staff resent informed, confidential and supportive criticism when accompanied by practical means of improvement and even fewer resent informed praise of their achievements. Such functions are a vital part of the role of middle management, but there is a sense in which the recognition of difficulties and successes by the school as opposed to the department or year provides more help on the one hand, and more credit on the other. Staff may seek and deserve protection from parents, outside agencies, and even close but antagonistic colleagues, and seek such support from senior colleagues; they may need the confidence to develop their careers in other ways, and value the perceptions of more experienced colleagues with a wider vision than their immediate manager. They may find it easier to discuss a weakness with someone they recognise as being successful and somewhat removed from the specific circumstances. Most of all, they need the reassurance that they are respected for their overall contribution to the school, and not simply each separate aspect of their work.

One very important function that senior management can perform on behalf of newly arrived staff, whether they be probationers or more experienced, and then continue performing during their time in the school, is that of getting them involved in more than simply teaching their timetabled commitment and discharging those tasks and duties laid down in their role definition and job specification. So much of what happens in a school relies on the initiatives and energies of staff in promoting extra-curricular activities and a lively school needs a dynamic that requires change in response to new demands. Where staff have ideas and energies that they wish to devote to these activities there can be real inhibitions to doing anything about them. Apart from those whose personalities consign them to taking a back seat, many feel that to push themselves forward will appear presumptuous, and may upset those already involved. This is especially true when matters of policy are involved. Newcomers are normally loath to make positive contributions. Senior management can, with a clear objective of getting staff involved and committed to the school, invite and encourage new colleagues to join in. The Head in our very first case study makes a considerable impact on our young probationary teacher when she invites him to share in activities outside the immediate work of his department. She shows that she is aware of his presence and recognises his worth, even though he has seen relatively little of her during his first year (p.26). Asking a probationer to become a member of a working party on 'Reporting to Parents' or to help with examination arrangements may add physical pressures in a busy year, but enables fresh ideas to find expression and provides the opportunity to meet with staff outside the department or faculty. It enhances status, lifts morale and, above all, recognises that professional worth is not the product of time-serving. What is true of the working party is also true of the many varied aspects of school life to which people need to be invited and that invitation needs to be undertaken, or confirmed by the most senior to avoid the feeling that to be so involved is self-aggrandisement. Such a role contrasts with that still prevalent in schools where the senior staff are on watch for 'empire-building', eager to deter those who would interfere in the business of other departments or years, reminding new arrivals that they do not appreciate the background to present policies and reasserting at every opportunity that valid ideas are only respected if they come from those of appropriate standing and experience. Thus, even though staff, from time to time, may be advised to keep the extent of their involvement within their physical capacity to cope with undue stress, the climate is determined by the Head and his or her close colleagues. If they choose, they can involve, not exclude, welcome, not freeze out, those who want to play their part.

Less senior staff are also very dependant on their more senior colleagues for advice and suggestions about the pace and direction of their career development. Many staff, especially if they recognise that there is a climate in the school which is conducive to such limitations, will seek out those whose position and experience seem to offer something valuable, and ask about what promotion they might reasonably seek and when. Frequently, the first step would, in fact, have to come from the senior member of staff. The impact of a Head or Deputy, who is seen to have been successful in climbing the professional ladder, searching out a colleague, and putting to him or her that they should be contemplating the next move, can be very great indeed. At times, of course, the senior staff's role may be to dissuade, or slow down, or divert; almost always it will be to recommend practical things to do to increase prospects. The experienced teacher who is seeking to develop a career in the difficult professional climate of today is presented in the case study entitled 'Development'. He seeks the advice and support of the Head who is responsible for his reference when he returns from an unsuccessful interview. The Head has positive suggestions to make in this very difficult situation (p.106). This is such an important aspect of senior management that a rapidly expanding number of schools are programming career development discussions into a formal structure, planned, recorded and referred back to each year. These discussions will often contain observations by junior colleagues about the way senior staff are doing their job, and thus help the senior staff to do that job more effectively. The main result is the support, encouragement and guidance that senior management gives to the rest of the staff.

The role of senior management in external relations

Senior management is seen by other staff as playing a dominant role in determining the style and character of the professional relationships within a school. They give a lead which will be followed, however reluctantly, by others. Staff also rightly expect senior management to play a vital part in influencing the public image of the school. In many ways, the task of the teacher is affected by the perceptions held by the local community, including the Education Authority, about the way the school tackles its job, and about the quality of its performance. All staff will influence this, but senior staff, through the extent that they create and sustain a public image, will carry the major responsibility. The case study 'Reputation' illustrates this important area of public relations. Parents are taking a greater interest and seeking a greater share in the running of schools and senior management must expect to face similar questions to those faced by this Head and her staff concerning the quality of teaching and the success or otherwise of the pupils in public examinations (p.98). Class teachers who experience difficulty in gaining access to local firms or farms, tutors who need the help of support agencies, or teachers who need assistance with curricular development schemes – all will benefit from a successful public image and the Head and his closest associates need to work to achieve this. Parents who are generally confident in the school's ability to do its job well will be more supportive and less resistant to staff who seek their help when tackling a student's problems.

In all these ways, senior staff, including the Head, have a direct part to play in establishing the conditions for successful teaching and learning; therein lies their principle function and justification. There is, however, more to their role than that. It has become traditional to see such staff as the administrators, meaning that they decide what is to be done and then see that systems are devised and operated to achieve these ends. Deputies frequently undertake such tasks as substitution rotas for absent colleagues, examination procedures, registration checks, furniture allocation and reprographics control; they may administer accounts, organise duty rotas, devise the layout for Parents Evenings, issue fire regulations, supervise assemblies and authorise bus passes. That these are necessary tasks is not disputed and they may indeed represent light relief for senior staff, but they may be accomplished with equal success by junior colleagues or even, in some cases, by non-teaching staff, as is witnessed by the fact that they are undertaken by such staff in some schools. Therefore, senior management is not justified because it takes on administrative tasks. Many of these can, and should, be done by junior staff who will gain greatly from the experience. It is a better use of senior staffs' skills if they are more involved in the teaching and learning situations and less constrained by routine tasks performed in offices away from children.

The job specifications of senior managers: varying the role

Finally, from the point of view of the senior management themselves, there are further aspects to their role than simply that of supporting their colleagues in their teaching tasks and providing personal support and counselling. Experienced staff need their own satisfactions and these can be seen as arising from playing a part in the development of students, the development of staff, and the extent to which the school is successful in meeting the changing needs of the society it serves. It is doubtful that the commonly held view that the Head is a generalist with overall responsibility, flanked by a number of specialists in, say, pastoral care, academic matters, resources or pupils' welfare, is an adequate model for the needs of a modern comprehensive school, or for the needs of the people fulfilling such roles.

Senior staff, for their own well-being and to avoid stress, need varied roles, in which there is a balance of different types of responsibility. A role that consists entirely of relating to people, especially when there is trouble, can exact a high price from that individual and there is merit in having elements in one's job brief that are simple to perform, do not include handling people and can be accomplished in a short time so that they can be seen to have been done. The Deputy who insists on arranging the examination desks in the Hall may be seeking such a small reward even though the task could be easily undertaken by the most junior colleague. In so far as many will aspire to Headship they need the opportunity of access to the full range of experiences that schools have to offer. Otherwise, the specialist Deputy or senior teacher lacks the range demanded by Headship. Further, and especially if movement is to continue to slow down between schools and into new jobs, they need the prospect of variety. These considerations suggest a job specification that is wide, varied, and capable of change. Too often, job specifications are elaborate schemes to keep out intruders, rather than devices for others to enjoy interesting experiences. Perhaps there is much to be gained by each senior manager designing their own balanced and varied brief, and re-negotiating it from time to time.

Senior staff need the access to young people that is not always prefaced by crisis or misdemeanour. They need to teach and enjoy the company of students free from disciplinary or administrative demands. They may need to find time to produce a play, look after a team, teach several classes and take groups out of school. They also need the framework that encourages staff to see them as worth confiding in. Part of the satisfaction of senior staff lies in the role they can play in enhancing the careers of their more junior colleagues. Thus all senior staff should make a contribution to a staff development programme, not only because they can help others, but so that they can gain personal satisfaction. Senior staff need a facility to be able to relax in the company of those with similar responsibilities to gain mutual support, share perceptions and discuss judgements. To be accessible they need a secure place in the staffroom, but also they need to meet their peers both informally and formally. Equally important, this contact should extend to those in a similar role in other schools. Frequently, meetings exist for Heads but less often does this possibility occur for Deputies and senior teachers. Yet not only does such provision provide encouragement and ideas, it also enables senior staff to gain a more balanced view as to the state of health and degree of success of that school. All too rarely do staff get the chance to visit other schools with the prime purpose of using the visit to assess the strengths and weaknesses of their own school. Similarly, they need to have opportunities to meet, professionally, with those elements of society that the school relates to; getting out of school to talk to employers, the police, social services, the local churches, groups of old age pensioners or the Chamber of Trade. Those who are charged with the responsibility for the effectiveness of the school need to seek perceptions from outside.

Senior management as a team

Above all, senior staff need the sense that they are part of a team. They have responsibility for the whole school, and yet they are often given specific roles that deny them legitimate access to extensive areas of school life. They need the collective strength that is available to a new teacher on joining a thriving department, or a tutor who belongs to a year group. They need others to check their ideas and actions, correct their prejudices, and counsel against undue worry or effort. In short, they need the sort of job specification that enables them to see the whole school working, and the support of colleagues who work with them in all that they do. If that sense of a team is not created, the tension and separation at senior level that result will be a powerful determinant of a tense and divided school.

Summary

Senior staff are, by definition, the most potentially influential staff in a school. Their enjoyment and effectiveness not only mould the immediate but also the next generation, for those that aspire to senior positions learn from their example. If senior staff are seen as the law-makers, making decisions for others to implement, escaping from the classroom, tired and even cynical about education, intent on stopping, interfering with or impeding initiatives, their power may strangle a school, blighting a population of students who have but one secondary school experience and obscuring their professional colleagues' vision of what can be achieved. If they are seen as the executives, implementing the decisions of all, escaping into the classroom, excited and challenged by education, intent on promoting, permitting and searching for initiatives, they have the immense satisfaction of working in a growing school, enriching the student population, and fostering an open, developing relationship with their professional colleagues.

Suggestions for further reading

BUSH, T. *et al* (eds) (1980) *Approaches to school management* (London, Harper and Row).
GLATTER, R. (1982) *Developing Staff for school management* Block 6, Part 6 of Open University Course E323 (Milton Keynes, Open University Press).
JOHN, D. (1980) *Leadership in Schools* (London, Heinemann Educational Books).
MORGAN, C. *et al* (1983) *The Selection of Secondary Headteachers* (Milton Keynes, Open University Press).
PETERS, R.S. (ed) (1976) *The Role of the Head* (London, Routledge and Kegan Paul).

References

HANDY, C. B. (1985) *Taken for Granted. Understanding Schools as Organisations* (London, Longman)

Chapter 11

Case Studies: Participation

1. Forum: the issue of how the distribution of a capitation allowance is dealt with by participative decision making

The head of the History department took a number of brown envelopes and pieces of paper from the pigeon-hole which bore his name. He thumbed through them while sipping his cup of coffee and his eye fell on a single slip of paper headed 'Forum – Agenda'. There was only one item on it: 'Distribution of the Capitation Allowance'. To a newly appointed member of the staff, the word 'forum' had a quaint classical ring about it, recalling the study of Latin many years ago, or more recently, a camping holiday in Italy. It still seemed a strange word to use for the main decision-making body of a large comprehensive school. At his interview last summer, the forum had been referred to and he gathered that as a head of department he would be expected to attend. He had not taken that much notice and had thought of it as the fancy name for the meeting of heads of departments which he had been used to at his previous school. However, he had gradually come to realise that this was a very different form of organisation from any which he had experienced in his career so far.

He first became aware of this soon after his arrival in September when a fairly substantial document entitled 'Capitation Allowance: report and proposals of the working party', appeared in his pigeon-hole. On the same day a lively young member of his department who was sharing a non-teaching period, flourished his copy of the document and informed him of some of the background to it. Apparently, mutterings and complaints about the existing system had begun to grow during the previous school year. As financial cuts had begun to bite, there was increasing discontent with the method whereby the capitation allowance was distributed by the decree of the senior mangement with little or no opportunity for discussion. Consequently, a working party had been set up to look into the whole matter and to come up with proposals which would be discussed at a meeting of the forum early in the autumn term. All this seemed admirable as a consultative process. What came as a surprise to him was to learn that the young member of his department expressed his intention of being at this meeting of the forum because it was a topic about which he felt strongly. He soon realised that any member of the staff was entitled to attend such a meeting – to take part in the discussion and to share in the decision making. Furthermore, it was at the forum that all major decisions of school policy took place. At his previous school he had been used to a fairly orthodox organisation. All major decisions (and many minor ones) had been taken by the senior management team which was composed of the Head, the three Deputy Heads and the three senior teachers. There had always been a good deal of consultation with the heads of departments and the heads of years, but there was no doubt where the important decisions were taken. In this school the situation was radically different. There was a senior management team, to be sure, but their role was largely an executive one. Major decisions were taken by the forum and he was anxious to see how it worked.

Meanwhile, during the fortnight before the meeting there was considerable discussion and argument in the staffroom about the proposals. There were three proposals of alternative methods to distribute the capitation allowance.

1. The first proposal left things largely as they were. The senior management team worked out the budget and presented it to the forum for approval or modification.
2. The second proposal was in the form of an arithmetical formula which was based upon the number of pupils taught and the number of periods taught by a particular department. It was an objective scheme based upon pupil-contact.
3. The third proposal was that each department put forward detailed estimates of its requirements. These were made public before the meeting of the forum which then discussed the combined estimates and made decisions.

The Deputy Head (Resources) made no secret of the fact that he would be very glad to get this matter sorted out as he had been on the receiving end of the resentment that had been expressed increasingly vehemently by certain individual members of staff and by certain departments over the previous year. To some it appeared that arbitrary cuts in their allowances had been made without any good reason, in spite of the strenuous efforts which had been made to explain to individual heads of departments that cuts had been made by the Local Education Authority which had to be passed on. The working party which he had chaired had taken a lot of evidence and had spent many long hours in arriving at its report and proposals. He would like to see the matter resolved, preferably in a way which would be fairly easy to administer.

The topic certainly aroused the interest of a number of the young members of the teaching staff too, and typical of these was a young economist who had been somewhat sceptical of his ability to influence the decisions in a large organisation. On this particular issue he felt particularly strongly and made every effort to persuade his colleagues to attend this meting of the forum and to make their feelings known. After all, if they did not attend, they could not complain afterwards that the decisions taken did not suit them. Besides, it was not a good thing that the 'old man' and 'the six wise men and women' (as he referred to the senior management team) should have their own way, when the opportunity existed for others to have a say. He had attended one or two meetings during his first year in the school and while some of the discussion had passed over his head, nevertheless it was interesting to be there when certain decisions were taken. He felt he understood better why, for example, Personal and Social Education was now taught throughout the school because he had been there when it had been decided. He had even found himself defending it to others who were sceptical of its value in the curriculum.

The meeting of the Forum took place after school and the head of History who was attending for the first time was interested in the attendance. All the heads of departments and heads of years as well as the senior management team were expected to be present, but in addition there was a substantial sprinkling of younger teachers and it was quite a large meeting. The Head was in the chair and after one or two brief pieces of information had been given relating to forthcoming open days and end-of-term functions, the main topic of the meeting was introduced, namely, the distribution of the capitation allowance.

The Deputy Head (Resources) spoke about the working party report and outlined how the three proposals had emerged from their discussions. He outlined the areas of dissatisfaction, particularly the very general feeling that once a budget containing figures had been tabled there was really very little room for manoeuvre or possibility for discussion. Any further bids involved taking money away from other departments and this could be a very acrimonious process. He expressed his own preference for the 'formula' proposal which was objective and easy to administer. It did not involve him or his colleagues in the senior management team in taking sides or showing bias. It was simple. There was strong support for this proposal from the larger departments, in particular from the English department, which, of course, had large contact time with pupils. On the other hand, the Science department, with a high rate of breakable consumables like test tubes, stressed that all lessons were not equally expensive. A number of the older and more conservative senior staff clearly wanted things to stay as they were. Surely, the senior management team were paid to take decisions like these. After all, they had the experience and could take a global view. It was some time before the younger members of staff became involved in the discussion, but eventually the vocal economist intervened. Although he did not say so, he felt that already the older and more senior members of the staff had had far too much influence on the meeting. Besides, they were missing the point that somehow an opportunity should be found for more people to influence important decisions such as this which affected everyone. The meeting began to gain momentum and the Head, while holding the ring, began to make his presence felt with some persuasive argument as well as summing-up from time to time.

The head of History, feeling rather shy to jump into the discussion at his first meeting was asking himself whether there was any difference between this meeting and others which he had attended at other schools. He soon decided that there was, because here was a major item of policy being discussed by a real cross-section of the staff including some of the most junior teachers. What remained to be seen was how any decisions would be arrived at.

A significant contribution came from the Art and Craft department when a young teacher argued that the discussion was not really about money but about the 'value' of subjects in the curriculum. Like many teachers of Art he felt that his subject was 'disadvantaged'. It lacked prestige, came off badly in option schemes, was taught to more of the less able pupils and received less money compared with Science or Technology even though it required expensive pieces of equipment like kilns for pottery and large amounts of consumable material.

Noises were made from various quarters about the importance of 'give and take' but the head of Special Education pointed out sharply

that some departments were in a better position to give than others
and the principle was fine until she was asked to surrender a
proportion of her meagre allowance and deprive children who were
already deprived.

Nevertheless, examples were quoted by the head of the third year,
of cases quite recently when some departments which had been in
difficulties because they were launching new courses had received
help from others who were established. Personal and Social
Education was a case in point and she had been most appreciative of
the help which she had received when developing this course in her
year.

The Deputy Head who had presented the proposals began to
recognise that there was weakening support for his relatively simple
arithemetical solution based upon pupil contact. Because of the
different equipment and materials used by, say, Geography as
compared with Science, some lessons really did cost more than others
and inevitably the bids of certain departments were bound to be
higher than others. What seemed important was that departments
should have the opportunity to make their bids and that these bids
should be made public so as to avoid the secretive 'cloak and dagger'
methods adopted in some schools. Also it seemed important that all
the money should be on the table and not some of it held back for
'contingencies', which often meant that patronage was left to the
Head or to the senior management. He would argue for the third
proposal which seemed to be gathering support round the room.

The head of History was struck by another characteristic of the
meeting which contrasted with his experiences in other schools – the
low-key nature of the discussions. There were occasional flashes of
conflict, but in the main the discussion lacked rhetorical speeches or
histrionic performances. The Head's style of chairmanship
contributed to this but was not entirely responsible for it. The
atmosphere was very relaxed, forenames were used, even when
addressing the Head, and there was a certain amount of humour even
when forceful points were being made. Junior teachers did not seem
in awe of the senior management or to show undue deference towards
them. Entrenched positions were not being defended stubbornly and
there was already some movement in the meeting towards a
consensus. He began to ask himself not which of the proposals he
would stand out for but which one was likely, in the long run, to
command the most support and the greatest respect.

The young economist was disappointed at how few of his junior

colleagues had spoken, but was encouraged by the support his own
views had received from an unexpected quarter, the rather
conservative number two in the Mathematics department who was
taking early retirement. Perhaps his imminent departure was
broadening his mind!

By now the meeting had gone on for quite a long time and the head
of History was becoming conscious of some fidgeting and of glances at
watches around the table. The Head too seemed sensitive to this
evident feeing that the meeting had gone on quite long enough. He
did not, however, move swifty to a premature or 'forced' consensus
but instead began to sum up slowly the discussion which had taken
place, pausing frequently for modification or clarification of a point,
inviting further contributions, allowing one or two people a final
word, not hurrying the latter stages of the meeting. Eventually, and
without sounding solemn or portentous he looked slowly round the
room and asked quietly whether there was a consensus in favour of
the third proposal. There were murmurs of assent. It was all very
undramatic.

On his way home in the car, the head of History reflected on his first
forum meeting. He felt satisfied that a good solution had been arrived
at. Some people had undoubtedly had to compromise their positions
but his feeling was that a meeting, a group of people rather than
individuals, had come to a decision. Why was it all so good-natured? It
must be something to do with the climate, the atmosphere, the quality
of human relationships in the school, which he was only just
beginning to get to know. It was also something to do with
involvement and motivation. People are more likely to be committed
to decisions in which they have shared than to those handed out to
them from above. He also found that he was asking himself the
question, 'What does this style of decision-making have to say to me
about the way I conduct my departmental meetings?'. He had once
heard one of the Deputies respond to a question about the aims of the
forum by saying that one of its purposes was staff development. He
had also heard a young Home Economics teacher describe the school
soon after his arrival, as 'comfortable and vital'. After the meeting of
the forum he felt that he understood a little better what each of them
had meant.

2. Decision making: a decision on whether to become involved in a TVEI scheme is taken in a hurry

At the beginning of September, Keith Gilman, the Head of Holly Bank High School was spending a day in school on his return from his summer holiday. His secretary had, as usual, separated the routine mail that could be dealt with quickly by telephone or by a dictated note from those letters which needed more careful consideration. One letter from the L.E.A. office gave him particular cause for concern. It was brief and referred to the government plans to extend their Technical and Vocational Education Initiative (TVEI). He was asked in the letter whether the school wished to be included in the Authority's bid for funding. An answer was required by the end of the month and if the school wished to participate it was expected to make a formal submission by 10th November so that the Authority could submit its own bid to the Manpower Services Commission by the required date. Furthermore, the submission from the school was to cover no more than one side of A4 paper and be in a form which could be sent to parents informing them of new courses which would be available to their children.

Keith looked at the calendar and pondered on the time-scale. Like so many things nowadays it was all happening very quickly. There seemed very little time in which to take the first decision if there was to be much in the way of consultation, let alone any participation. Keith was commited to the notion of participation and had introduced a participative system of decision-making when he was appointed ten years ago. Responsibility for all major policy decisions lay with the forum which all members of the teaching staff had the right to attend. The system worked reasonably well and most members of staff now expected to play a part in planning policy. However, the new term did not start until the following week. The decision whether to bid for a TVEI extension was an important one involving a large amount of money to meet the cost of staffing and equipping new courses if the school were to take part. It was certainly an issue that would normally go before the forum for full discussion prior to a decision being taken. Was there time for all that?

While Keith was thinking over the problem, there was a knock on his door and Mary Horton, one of his Deputies, looked in. After swapping some holiday experiences and comments on the results in external examinations Keith handed her the letter. Mary was a physicist and of a pragmatic frame of mind. She smiled as she read it.

'Well, what are you going to do? Say yes?'

'I don't know yet', said Keith, 'I suppose it will have to go to the forum'. Mary paused and then said,

'Is there time for that? I should say yes, Keith. We need the money. My department will be delighted.'

'You know how I feel about deciding things without involving other people', replied Keith.

'Well involve them', Mary countered 'tell the other deputies, like you've told me, get the consent of the faculty heads, and give the L.E.A. your answer. Then all you've got to do is to appoint a coordinator to prepare the submission.'

'And what about the forum'? Keith asked.

'You will just have to tell them there wasn't time for all the usual procedures. After all they will have the chance to discuss the submission once the coordinator has drawn it up. They will take part in approving that. There's your precious participation. And now, I must fly and catch the garden centre before lunch.'

Mary left hurriedly and Keith was left still looking thoughtful with the letter in his hand.

Keith Gilman was somewhat stubborn by nature and didn't like being hustled, particularly by his L.E.A. He spent a couple of days thinking over his problem and comparing it in his mind with other issues over which major decisions had been taken. He made his mind up. The forum would decide.

Before term started, assisted by his deputies, he prepared a pack of papers for every member of staff. This included background papers on TVEI and details of existing schemes in the L.E.A. These documents were in the staff pigeon-holes on the day before term began. The original letter from the L.E.A. was published in the first staff bulletin. A meeting of the forum was arranged for a week later. The Authority's TVEI Coordinator and the Senior Adviser were invited to attend to answer questions.

In the usual turmoil of starting a new school year this caused some disturbance and confusion. Most subject departments held hasty impromptu meetings, there were some misunderstandings and many questions. Keith received a number of visits from heads of subject departments seeking further information. Does it apply to us? How soon will it start? Why the hurry? What's different about MSC money? About 35 per cent of the staff, the usual proportion, attended the meeting of the forum. Many questions were asked and the following discussion lasted about two hours. As usual the meeting was rather low key in tone. Most people were seeking information, looking for advantages, financial or otherwise and seeking the snags, particularly the objections and effects on the existing curriculum. Who would gain and who would lose out? Slowly, and not without difficulty, a consensus was arrived at to take part in the scheme.

Keith was pleasantly surprised but this was only the beginning. The submission now had to be worked out. The details of the meeting were published in the next staff bulletin. Five working parties were set up, composed of volunteers, convened but not chaired by members of senior management. They were to look at the following crucial areas and report in two weeks.

1. Information technology.
2. Residential and work experience.
3. Profiling and records of achievement.
4. Courses to be offered in the fourth and fifth years.
5. Staffing and resources.

The following two weeks were hectic. On top of all their other work of preparing lessons, teaching and marking, members of the working parties read, talked and visited other schools. There was again some confusion but by now considerable enthusiasm was beginning to appear. Some staff were sceptical, others remained puzzled. The senior management made a suggestion that the staff devoted the whole of an in-service training day in October to this issue and after something of a last-minute scramble the working parties produced their reports for circulation to all members of the staff in time for that day.

The in-service training proved very valuable in helping to clarify the thinking of many people and to harness the interest of others who had been apathetic. More people began to realise that there was something in it for them. There was discussion in groups of all the papers followed by a meeting of the forum in the afternoon. What was becoming apparent by then was that the staff, or a large number of them, were beginning to 'own' this problem and were expressing a clear desire to use the TVEI experience as an opportunity to reappraise other aspects of the school's curriculum. The climate was ready. They were not simply going to add on a TVEI element to the existing programmes. They were willing to accept a radical reorganisation of the curriculum and to manipulate this large injection of money to their advantage and more especially to the advantage of young people. At the end of this meeting it was suggested that the Head should write the submission in the light of the day's discussions. As one wit put it:

'You are the only one with time to do things like that'.

Keith wrote the submission that evening when he got home after a meeting of the P.T.A. committee and published it in the staff bulletin two days later. The forum met again a week later and with some minor modifications the submission was approved and sent off to the L.E.A. on 9 November.

At the end of the month the senior management team were having their weekly meeting and considering the task they had been commissioned by the forum to tackle.

'As I see it', said Jack Fulford, the second Deputy and chairman of the curriculum sub-committee, 'we have a major curriculum review on our hands in the next six months.'

'Yes', added Mary Horton, 'I wouldn't have believed we could be where we are now, if you told me at the beginning of term. It was all a bit breathless, wasn't it'?

Keith Gilman smiled ruefully, 'I don't mind telling you I was just as confused as everyone else most of the time. I suppose it was the pressure of time, the deadlines, all the other day-to-day chores that kept getting in the way.'

Jack looked across at the Head, 'But that's the way it is now. It's very tempting to simply say yes or no and leave it at that when the L.E.A., the government, MSC, or anybody else throws things at us.'

Jack paused. 'Interesting though, wasn't it, how the staff came round to it.'

Mary put in, 'I'm sure all those visits helped a lot, got people involved, in spite of themselves.'

Keith laughed, 'Yes, it's funny how people react. About a month ago Jerry Arnold stopped me in the corridor and said "Why on earth don't you handle this TVEI thing, Keith? You know all about it." Then at the end of the last forum meeting he came up and said grudgingly, "You've got us all mixed up in this business of the curriculum now, haven't you? I don't know how you manage it."

3. The origins, constitution and activities of a participative system of decision making is illustrated from a school where it has operated for many years

The following is an extract from the Staff Brochure for Marple Ridge High School, Stockport. The school was established as an 11–18 coeducational comprehensive school in 1974, with students and many staff coming initially from two small single-sex secondary modern schools. These members of staff, with those who joined the school in its early years, worked with the incoming Head to create a management style characterised by each teacher having access to the entire policy-making for the school and by the maximum degree of autonomy for faculties and year teams. Class teachers and senior staff were charged with seeing that the policy was implemented.

The particular structures described here, modified and refined over recent years, are less important than the underlying purposes which they seek to serve. These have been explained as ensuring that all staff, teaching and non-teaching, and now numbering nearly 100 in all, feel involved in the success of the school, gain a sense of commitment to the school and its students, and grow in confidence in delivering the curriculum.

SENIOR MANAGEMENT GROUP
(The head, three deputy heads and three senior teachers)

This Group is charged with ensuring the effective and efficient organisation of the school for the benefit of all who make up the community, and to the satisfaction of all, including the Local Authority and the Department of Education and Science. The Group meets once a week, with other meetings when necessary, and any member of the school may bring to the attention of the Group any matter which they wish to see discussed. The Group will make decisions where appropriate, submit proposals to the Board, an Open Staff Meeting or to individuals, and help implement and evaluate the policies previously adopted.

An overriding principle of the Group's operation is that of collective responsibility and, therefore, although each member of the Senior Management Group has a specific area of responsibility, any student or member of staff may approach any member of the Group on any matter. Often it will be essential to have a matter resolved speedily and the nearest person is the most appropriate one to contact. The member contacted will ensure that the incident is reported to the member responsible. Each member liaises with Heads of Faculty, with regard to curriculum planning and development, the devising of options and teaching methods, and Heads of Year with regard to any aspect of the well-being of their year group.

THE BOARD

1 This body is the principal policy-making body of the School; all matters of concern to everyone have been or can be debated here and if the Board can reach a consensus, then that consensus represents official policy and is included in the next Staff Brochure. Its deliberations are reported in the weekly bulletin, as is its Agenda.

2 The Board was set up in 1973 to enable as wide a range of staff as possible to participate in the decision-making process for the newly re-organised Comprehensive School opening in September 1974. It arose out of full meetings of all staff, both teaching and non-teaching, owes its origin and power to such a meeting, and remains subservient to the whole staff. Its function is to provide a representative meeting, smaller and therefore more easily convened, yet accessible to all.

3 Membership of the Board is the S.M.G., all Heads of Faculty and all Heads of Year, or their representatives, plus any other member of staff, teaching or non-teaching, who wishes to attend. Invitations have been extended from time to time to interested visitors, students and the Chairman of Governors. Normal attendances are approximately 30.

4 Meetings are, by tradition, held in the Lower School Staffroom, begin at 4.00 p.m. and end at 5.15 p.m., or later with the permission of the meetings. They are invariably held on a Monday, and usually occur twice a term or more often if business requires it.

5 Meetings of the Board are chaired by the Head, or by another member of the S.M.G. in his absence. The Head performs several functions:
   a He endeavours to keep the Board informed about all matters relating to its business, including any constraints imposed by D.E.S. or L.E.A. or Governors' policy.
   b He aims to ensure full, free and open debate, in which he may join as appropriate, i.e. he is not a neutral Chairman.
   c He tests various proposals, often offered by other members, to see if a consensus can be achieved.
   d He retains the responsibility of seeing that policy exists and is implemented.

6 Meetings are most successful when they deal with a single item on the Agenda, though it is often necessary to take the opportunity to deal with brief business relating to other matters at the beginning of the meeting.

7 Meetings may, at the outset, be designated as general discussion, without any attempt to reach a decision, or may attempt to reach a decision but agree to hold another meeting to allow time for further consideration, or may fail to reach an agreement. If no consensus is deemed possible, the meeting may agree that the matter be referred to a vote of the whole staff, teaching or non-teaching, specifying the need for a two-thirds majority for a major change of policy, or a simple majority for a less significant change, or the meeting may call upon the Head or S.M.G. to arbitrate.

8 The Head does not retain a veto on policy decisions; any policy commanding the support of the rest of the meeting should command his support also, and this applies to all those who attend.

9 Matters to be discussed by the Board may be suggested by any member of staff; it is generally held that the Board should not discuss matters that lie outside its power to act, nor should it seek to make decisions which properly belong to Faculties, Year teams or individual teachers, i.e. it should only take action when it is necessary rather than seek to control all aspects of the school.

10 To avoid the waste of staff energies on unprofitable endeavours, it is usually the case that the Board is first asked to authorise a Working Group, indicating in advance that it would welcome advice in the form of a report reviewing opinions, examining alternatives and recommending action after seeking views as widely as time will allow. (Major policy decisions rarely require sudden action; most benefit from careful thought and the school tries not to be lead by 'crisis' management.) Membership of the Working Group is open to anyone who volunteers.

11 Working Group Reports are circulated to all the staff to allow Faculty and Year discussions and to the S.M.G. prior to a Board Meeting. The S.M.G. will make a positive response at the Board, though this does not imply that any individual reservations or ideas held by a member of the S.M.G. will not be expressed at the Board.

12 Interpretation of School Policy is in the hands of the S.M.G., and all staff are expected to observe both school policy and S.M.G. interpretations. However, all S.M.G. actions may be subject to questioning by individual enquiry, attendance by a member of staff at the weekly S.M.G. meeting, comment from a meeting of Heads of Faculty or Heads of Year, Faculty or Year meetings, Union Representation or debate at the Board. It must be recognised, however, that some policy matters are not determined by the school, e.g. admissions policy, suspension policy etc. Staffing structures and appointments, after allowing for full consultation, are determined by the Head, S.M.G. and L.E.A.

13 The Board is a vital instrument for ensuring that the school operates by consent of all its staff, enabling everyone, whatever their position, to contribute ideas and opinions, to achieve change by debate and persuasion rather than riding roughshod over minority opinions, avoiding the vagaries of dictatorial pronouncements by one person or a small group, without encouraging anarchy or woolly-minded oscillations in policy.

Questions for discussion

'Forum' (pp.131-36)

1. In what ways does the meeting described contrast with meetings which you have attended in your school? Are there meetings that perform a similar function?
2. Discuss the style of leadership exercised by the Head as chairman of this meeting.
3. In what ways does 'climate' influence the process and outcome of this meeting? How is the 'climate' of a meeting created?
4. How is consensus arrived at in a meeting of this kind? In what other ways can a meeting come to a decision? Discuss the advantages and disadvantages of the various means of reaching a decision.
5. How do you distinguish between a consultative and a participative process of decision making?
6. Not all meetings are as well behaved as the one described. Discuss ways of resolving conflict in meetings. What skills of chairmanship are needed in handling conflict in meetings?
7. If you were a young teacher at this school would you have bothered to attend this meeting? Discuss the part that can be played by junior teachers in major school decisions.
8. As a head of department would you be able to adopt a participative style of chairmanship at your departmental meetings? Would you see any merit in doing so?
9. What would you do as a Head if the forum reached a consensus which you did not feel that you could support?

'Decision making under pressure' (pp.137-40)

1. Discuss the Head's handling of this issue. How do you think it would have been handled in your school?
2. In what ways is a participative system more difficult to operate when demand for change comes from outside the school?
3. Discuss the role of the senior management team in this case study. As a Deputy Head would you have felt satisfied with the outcome?
4. What part do communications play in this case study? Discuss the various methods of communication available to a school.
5. Should any school staff meetings be built into the school timetable?

What benefits are there from devoting an in-service training day to
this issue? Can a day thus spent be justified as in-service training?
6 'Schools have no time to manage. They can either be run by
autocracy or by autonomy.' Discuss this statement.
7 Invite each member of your group to describe briefly how a major
policy decision was taken recently at his or her school and how the
decision affected staff morale.
8 What would be the effect on school decision making of appointing
Heads of secondary schools from outside the education service and
paid on separate salary scales to teachers?

'A participative management system operating in a school' (pp.141-43)

1. How does this structure differ from that operating in your school?
2. In paragraph no.8 of this document it states that 'the Head does
not retain a veto on policy decisions'. Can this be true? Are there
not some matters over which the Head must retain this right? If so,
what are they?
3. Can the senior management group provide effective leadership
and a sense of job satisfaction for all its members without
emphasising the distinctive role of each member.
4. What might be the inhibitions to a junior member of the staff
attending and contributing to the Board.

In-service project work

1. Devise a role play exercise based upon the meeting in the case
study 'Forum' to explore how consensus is arrived at.
2. Invite each member of your group to write a short letter to a Head
advocating or initiating change which will affect the school's
curriculum. In pairs role play as Head and Deputy a discussion on
how this matter is to be handled.
3. Devise an exercise in which a small team has to come to a decision
under pressure of time and which might be used in an in-service
training course for middle or senior managers.
4. Invite the manager of a local bank, a local business and a local
football team to discuss with your senior management team how
decisions are taken in different organisations.

Chapter 12

Determining Policy in Secondary Schools: A Participative Approach

We have considered managing for learning at three different levels in a secondary school and in this final chapter examine the structure for decision making and, in particular, the process of determining policy.

The traditional structure for decision making in secondary schools

There is a strong tradition within the English education system that the Head is in control of a school. This view originated in the autocratic style of many famous headmasters in the nineteenth century and still persists. Parents and outside agencies seeking a person to identify, often refer to the Head as decision-maker. With the growth in size of secondary schools a bureaucratic hierarchy has developed and many decisions are still taken by the Head alone or by the senior mangement team composed of the Head and Deputies. This is sometimes extended to include other senior teachers. Few Heads of secondary schools would now profess to operate an autocratic system in which they issue directives for others to follow. Most would probably claim that they run a consultative system in which in varying degrees they seek and receive the views of other staff before making major decisions. Along with a readiness to listen to, if not to take advice from, colleagues has gone the need to delegate a range of decisions to departmental or house/year levels. The dominant view, in these schools, and they are in the majority, is that policy comes from the top of the hierarchy but that policy is likely to be more reasonable, sensitive and acceptable because it has taken into account the views of those whom it will affect, or at least some of them. Both the autocratic and the consultative models represent an in-line approach where superior and subordinate have a defined relationship with each other and responsibility and authority are both clear cut.

Some secondary schools have seriously doubted whether either of the two hierarchical models are appropriate for the effective operation of the institution and have developed a participative or collegiate approach. This approach has its origins in the sameness of teachers rather than their differences and in the notion that we have supported throughout this book that all teachers are managers. All teachers have a similar educational background, albeit differentiated by subject specialisms, and a broadly similar professional experience in classrooms. Almost all senior staff and many Heads go on teaching, so continuing to share similar experiences with their colleagues throughout their careers. It is generally true that when teachers begin to take on major administrative roles, they do so without formal training. Thus, the situation in schools, unlike that in other organisations, is one in which fellow professionals perform broadly similar tasks, needing each other's cooperation and often without differentiated training.

Some schools, rejecting the concepts of hierarchy and in-line management have approached policy-making and decision-taking as a function of all the staff, not simply of the Head or the senior staff. The participative model is one where policy is in the hands of all the staff. The legislative function is not exercised by senior management but by all the teachers, who are seen as all being managers. The Head and senior colleagues in this model carry out an executive function; that is, they use their authority and experience to ensure that action follows policy making, that things happen, and that there is a policy when one is needed. The model emphasises that all teachers are professionals who have a contribution to make to the running of the school. It reflects their independence for they do behave independently and are unsupervised for most of the working day. It is appropriate to harness this autonomy into a corporate body and to arrive at all major decisions by involving all staff in the process. There is evidence that the participative system is more effective in handling decision making and policy making in two areas which are particularly relevant to the life of schools today. One such area is the establishing, monitoring and developing of a coherent school ethos which provides stability and continuity of values in a school, and the second area is in managing change, a constant feature of contemporary education. Handy (1985), in an unbiased view of school organisation seen from the standpoint of an industrial management specialist, considers the hierarchical 'role' culture inappropriate for bringing about change (p.12).

There needs to be a consultative mechanism which is open to all, a policy group which is representative of all, but which is linked with the executive. (p.37).

The forum is the body which, in our view expresses these vital functions in a secondary school and involves all the teachers in so doing. We have illustrated a meeting of this body in the case study 'Forum' in which the events are drawn from personal experience (p.131).

The case for participation (1): stability and continuity. Professional norms and school ethos

The traditions of professionalism in teaching are strong although they are not always clearly defined. We have already referred to the relationship between teacher and taught, considered by many to be sacrosanct. Teachers see themselves as responsible for young lives during a critical period of their development and many show a dedication and involvement far beyond their timetabled classes and other duties. They recognise that to be *in loco parentis* is sometimes an awesome and arduous task. These norms of responsibility and dedication are the basis of accountability to one's profession. They are the source of the independence and autonomy which teachers cherish *vis-à-vis* their colleagues. These professional norms exist outside the immediate confines of the school in which they teach and are brought to bear on various occasions during their professional lives, although not often talked about in classrooms. They lie behind attitudes which influence their behaviour towards children and influence their decisions on professional matters such as the appropriateness of mixed-ability teaching, school uniform and corporal punishment. These professional norms exist alongside the norms of the institution. The school, too, will have a set of values which characterises its ethos, culture or climate. Ethos is recognised by Rutter *et al* in 'Fifteen thousand hours' to be of considerable significance in the growth and health of an effective school. It is notoriously difficult to define or pin down but is an amalgam of the attitudes, beliefs, allergies, neuroses, heroes and villains of all who inhabit a school. However, such a concept is too vague and diffuse to be of practical value. If it is to influence young people in practical ways there must be some coherent expression of the values subscribed to by a majority of the teachers. Some values may be expressed in school brochures; others, as we saw in our first case study, are unwritten. However, those which are written down will be empty rhetoric unless borne out in day-to-day happenings in the schools. The way teachers talk to children, the way children are treated, the tones of voice used, all reveal what values characterise the school's ethos. Values can be taught and attitudes developed. This must remain a major element in the curriculum. The *11–16 Curriculum Project* (1983) in its final report stressed the importance of attitudes as well as concepts and skills in the curriculum of each subject. It was significant that when the 41 individual schools examined their curriculum they came up with a remarkably consistent set of values which a school should encourage its pupils to form. They were:

adaptability	tolerance
commitment	empathy
cooperation	consideration for others
reliability	curiosity
self-confidence	honesty
self-discipline	integrity
perseverance	

To teach the formation of such attitudes is a complex process, but the first item for 'Necessary Action' under this heading of 'Attitudes' is:

> to agree the definition of the words used so that *all* staff have a basis for discussion. (p.32).

The forum provides the mechanism for this process to take place.

It is genuinely very difficult for a school to match professional norms to the norms or culture of the school, to develop a coherent set of values and to present a consistent message to children and to their parents. Values such as we have discussed represent a stable and continuous element in the school's curriculum and attitudes become of even more vital importance when almost everything else in the sphere of knowledge and skills is changing rapidly. The pressures for change are manifest and much talked about, but what is often lost sight of is the need for a degree of stability and consistency in children's schooling. This is taught mainly through the ethos of the school, and in the circumstances and the society in which schools find themselves today it cannot be left to chance. It needs to be managed. When school remains the only place where many children find any stability or where positive values are taught or sought, then the

'hidden' curriculum cannot remain hidden: it must become overt.
The creation of a whole school ethos or climate is something in which
all teachers play a part, but in our view their participation in this
process cannot be left to happen – it needs to be built into the
decision-making structure as a formal meeting place or as we describe
it, a forum. This is the place where the school's ethos or value system is
developed, monitored, tested out in discussion and debate and kept
under constant review.

The case for participation (2): managing change in schools

Consistent values give a school stability and continuity. This is our first
justification for a participative system of decision-making.
Paradoxically, the second justification for participation lies in the
need for a structure which will be able to manage change effectively.
We do not mean a structure simply to implement change, to adopt
and put into practice every change with which schools are confronted
nowadays. The need is for a body of professionals in a school to face
possible changes from within the school and without, to test out and
assess those changes and take policy decisions as to how such
challenges are to be met. Not all changes will be welcome, not all will
be able to be afforded. There will need to be selection and there will
sometimes be rejection. We have provided a case study in which a
school is faced with just such a decision, whether to become involved
in a TVEI extension which will significantly influence the curriculum.

The changes which began a decade ago ushered in a new era of
change for secondary schools. They began with the moves to change
the curriculum. This was to be preceded by a process of curriculum
appraisal, a largely school-based activity. Accompanying this process
were changes originating in the demographic trends of falling school
rolls. These had a degree of inevitability about them. Far more
dramatic have been those changes thrust upon schools by the
government by a move towards greater centralisation in the education
service and by greater concern on the part of the public, parents and
employers about the quality of schooling. These changes have come
in the form of funding by the MSC of such initiatives as TVEI, by
attempts to match salary increases with tighter job specifications for
teachers, which control their conditions of service, and by social
pressures arising from the growth of a multi-cultural society. Such
changes have placed education and schools firmly in the political

arena and under continual public scrutiny by the media. School and
its curriculum is no longer the 'secret garden' where decisions can be
taken in a leisurely fashion and hidden from the public gaze. There is
tremendous pressure for schools to continue to remain an
authoritative and autocratic management structure, with a hierarchy
in which decisions which have been taken outside the school are
handed down to subordinates within it and any policy decisions which
are taken within the school are the responsibility of the senior
management. The demands for accountability to the government, to
the L.E.A. or to the governors are met by the Head being held
responsible and consequently taking many decisions personally or
after consultation with close colleagues. It is precisely in these
circumstances that a participative system provides an appropriate
mechanism for teachers to exercise their corporate professional
judgement in determining collectively what changes should take
place in a school.

A participative system for determining policy

In spite of the immediate pressures and the accompanying
temptations to persist with in-line management, steep hierarchies and
an autocratic style of leadership, there is now considerable evidence
that the conditions of change and prospects of more change are
precisely those for which the hierarchical and bureaucratic model is
inappropriate, particularly where the organisation is composed
largely of professionals.

McGregor's Theory Y (1960 and 1967) asserts that external control
and direction is not the only means of motivating people. The average
professional seeks and does not avoid responsibility and many more
people are able to contribute creatively to solving organisational
problems than do so. Likert (1967 and 1976) distinguishes four
systems of management. System 1 is exploitive and authoritative, and
is characterised by fear, threats, downward communication and
decision making at the top. System 2 is benevolent and authoritative;
management uses rewards, policy decisions are taken at the top and
some decision making may be delegated. System 3 is consultative and
encourages some involvement, with some communication up and
down and subordinates exerting some influence. System 4 is
characterised by participative group management in which superiors
and subordinates are close psychologically, decision making is by

group processes and is integrated into the formal structure by overlapping groups.

Handy (1985), directing his attention specifically at schools, stresses that the independence and autonomy beloved of professionals can only exist where there is strong and broadly based policy making:

> Schools close up their policy structure at their peril. (p.37).

While he does not claim that all staff have to take part in all decisions, nevertheless, they must all have the opportunity to contribute or dissent. He believes that schools, like all professional organisations, have to be run by consent, not command, and require policy structures which have mechanisms:

(a) for dredging-up ideas (working-parties, task forces and sub-committees), and

(b) for testing ideas (representative bodies, parliaments, moots) (p.37)

To this evidence we add personal experience of a participative system and contend that in the present climate there is an even greater need for the representative bodies, boards, forums or moots which can test, examine, appraise, select and, if necessary, reject ideas and proposals for change. There is a need, particularly in the present conditions of centralisation and outside pressures, for there to be a degree of tension between the internal policy makers of the school and the outside forces for change. This is provided by the forum. The case study on the TVEI submission illustrates the pressures under which school decision making now operates. It would have been easy and indeed tempting to take a quick decision in this case, but would the staff's commitment to the change have been so enthusiastic and would the quality of the changes from the young people's point of view have been the same?

The forum

The need to involve all professional teachers in developing and maintaining the continuity of the school's ethos and climate of values and the need for a policy structure for coping with change, in other words the need for a mechanism for taking all major decisions which is appropriate for a secondary school, leads us to advocate the forum, called by others a board, a council, a moot or a parliament. It is a

formal setting, a meeting which takes place regularly and which every
member of the teaching staff (and some would say, also the non-
teaching staff) has a right to attend, if they so wish. The forum is the
place of legislation and it has status, standing for and representing the
combined professionalism of the institution. All teachers have a right
and an opportunity to attend, to participate in the discussion, to share
in the debate and to be there when decisions are taken. They have the
opportunity to ask questions, to examine the views of others, to listen
to explanations, to put their own case and to match their wits. When
major decisions involving change have been taken there is a much
greater likelihood of commitment from people who were there when
the decisions were taken, a greater possibility that people will readily
become involved in the implementation of such decisions. The
constitution and function of the Board, as it is called, in our final case
study illustrates how this happens in a particular school where a
participative system has been in operation for many years. Handy
makes a further valuable point:

> If you participate in policy decisions you are generally happy to
> get on with your own thing, with a leader exercising oversight
> and an administrator providing the infrastructure. (p.37).

In the meetings of such a body decisions may be arrived at by voting
but more often they tend to emerge rather than to be taken. It is
seldom necessary to take a vote if all the possibilities and options have
been considered and openly canvassed. The search for consensus is a
process to which such a group becomes accustomed. A forum should
not be thought of as operating in a vacuum, suddenly meeting with an
agenda for which people are unprepared. The essence of its function
is as a formal manifestation of relationships which already exist in the
day-to-day life of the school. It will play a major part in the micropolitics of the institution. The formal meetings will be carefully
prepared beforehand, sometimes by papers, or working party
reports, always by gossip, by dealing, by lobbying and by all the
repertoire of negotiation.

The eventual meeting of the forum in the case study had been
prepared for by the circulation of proposals by a working party on
'Capitation Allowance' and by much previous discussion both in
subject department meetings and in the staffroom (p.132). The staff
facing the decision-making about committing the school to TVEI
received a pack of information about it, details of other schemes
operating in the L.E.A. and some teachers took the opportunity to
visit the schools where these schemes were taking place (p.139).

Leadership in a participative system

A typical reaction of many to whom participative decision-making is explained is that it is an abdication of responsibility on the part of the leader. If everyone shares in the decisions then who is the leader, in fact why have a leader? Surely, they say, participation by all is the negation of leadership? Certainly, participation requires a specific style of leadership and we would claim that leadership is not only as important as in any other system but more sophisticated, and probably more difficult. To promote or initiate a participative system, a Head requires a particular quality of confidence and a capacity for risk-taking. The leader leads from within what is often a large group. Particular skills are required to chair meetings of the forum. Although a head has status and authority, he or she may be vulnerable and feel very threatened when exposed to the pressures which a participative body can bring to bear. Consequently, there will be tension and possibly conflict to be resolved. Certainly, the role is subject to stress. The style also requires skill in listening, explaining, elucidating, summing up and recapitulating. The chairperson needs the skill to steer a course towards consensus, a sensitivity to atmosphere and a recognition of power groups. This, again, is the micropolitics of participation.

In the case study 'Forum', the Head's style is particularly commented upon. There is a relaxed atmosphere and there is some humour. The Head is sensitive to atmosphere and listens a lot. As he sums up, he clarifies, invites final comments, and does not hurry the meeting to a premature consensus.

It was all very undramatic. (p.136)

This view of leadership owes much to the work of Tannenbaum on participative management systems (1968).

Hierarchy is divisive, it creates resentment, hostility and opposition. Participation reduces disaffection and increases the identification of members with the organisation.

Tannenbaum claims that control in an organisation should not be thought of as a given quantity but as expandable so that everyone can have more of it. In a participative system the total amount of control is increased by more people taking part in decision making.

Paradoxically, through participation, management increases its control by giving up some of its authority.

A further dimension of leadership in a participative system is emphasised by Handy (p.31) when he indicates the role of the Head in creating a cohesive ethos.

> If independent professionals are to be linked together into a cohesive whole, the most natural way in which this can be done is through commitment to a cause.

He distinguishes 'transactional leadership', which involves the fixing and dealing which are necessary in administration and, we would say, in some negotiations, from 'transforming leadership' (from McGregor Burns, *Leadership*, 1978) which involves:

> Leaders and followers raising one another to higher levels of motivation, various words are used for such leadership: elevating, mobilising, inspiring, exalting, uplifting, exhorting . . .

This style of leadership provides one of the recipes for success advocated by Peters and Waterman in their *In Search of Excellence* (1983). It is 'hands on, value driven'.

Handy considers that such 'transforming leadership' welds together the school more effectively than any rule book. Throughout this book we have looked at management from the perspective of those who are managed and advocated a style of management which is supportive, in the belief that the management in schools exists to support those who are managing learning. To this we add the above notion of 'creative leadership' which is concerned to promote and sustain the values of the school, provide drive and chart a way into the future. The organisation of a secondary school is therefore characterised in our view by three factors: supportive management, creative leadership and a participative structure.

Other levels of participation

If the notion of the forum is valid and if a participative system is appropriate for taking major decisions in a secondary school then it is also appropriate at other levels of the school; for example, in pastoral groupings, and in subject departments. The model does not simply imply a structured meeting place where personal, professional and institutional values are brought together, but represents a particular quality of relationships which, once developed, animate the school at all levels.

The process whereby consensus is achieved is often complex, lengthy and sometimes tortuous, but it is characterised by mutual respect and recognition of the professionalism of colleagues. Certainly, there is no lack of conflict in such a process. It would be naïve to suggest that issues concerned with the shaping of young lives will not be debated with ardour and sometimes with passion at all levels. The appropriate leadership skill is in resolving such conflict and gaining consensus in conditions of difficulty and ambiguity. It may often involve clearing a way through a debris of argument towards the least unacceptable of a number of solutions. It may require a great deal of time and much patience. These skills may be exercised by a Head and equally by a head of a subject department. They will all require training in what is a sophisticated form of interpersonal relationships.

When all members of the teaching staff have the right and opportunity to attend the forum and participate in formulating policy then the role of a senior management team is clearly different from that undertaken in a traditional school. Instead of being the legislature, devising and legitimising policy, they are seen as the executive, implementing and monitoring policy laid down by the whole staff. Their tasks are to ensure that there are policies, that these policies are understood and that they are carried out. They will, of course, have been involved in decisions and their status and experience mean that their role is significant in any debate, but it is in the implementation of policy that they play a hierarchical and administrative role. This work is crucial and there is often an element of interpretation involved, but it is always subject to scrutiny, review and change by the forum.

Some benefits of participation

Participation is not a common feature of English secondary schools; in fact, as we have suggested, the current trend is towards greater centralisation, taking more policy decisions away from the school and placing them in the hands of the governors, the L.E.A. or the government. Nevertheless, it is our belief that it is precisely in these conditions that a participative system strengthens the school and enhances the professional status of all its teachers. Those who participate in decisions can claim ownership and involvement in those decisions. They will have greater understanding and a heightened awareness of problems facing a school. Greater awareness will not necessarily lead to consensus, indeed differences of view may be magnified by discussion. Schools contain a multiplicity of views and meeting to determine policy brings this into the open and may lead to greater cohesion. Decisions left in the hands of a few invite dissension, resentment and dissociation from the decision. Involvement in the decisions is more likely to lead to a commitment to their implementation. If people have played a part in deciding upon a policy concerning their subject, their department or their class, they are less likely to decline overtly or more often covertly to follow that development. A further benefit of a participative system is the pooling of expertise. Large secondary schools contain a wealth of knowledge and experience which can be tapped and a participative system facilitates access to the perceptions of new and junior staff. Good ideas are not the monopoly of senior staff. Participation engages more people in the search for solutions. The young economist in the case study 'Forum' played a not inconsiderable part in the meeting and was encouraged by the support his own views received from colleagues with more conservative views (p.135).

Some problems of participation

The most obvious problem of participation is the time taken to reach decisions. Important issues are best dealt with carefully and not in haste, but to enable all staff to become fully aware of such issues and to become involved in their resolution takes time. There is a danger that major decisions may be obstructed or at least delayed by a series of meetings to enable all to have their views considered. Reaching a consensus can be a protracted process and the time-scale can arouse impatience. At worst, setting up a working party to gather views and canvas possible solutions to a problem may be seen as a deliberate delaying tactic to put off a difficult decision.

There is also a limit to the energy of staff who are busy with the routine tasks of preparation, teaching, marking and reporting. Effort is required at the end of a working day to attend meetings, consider working-party reports, debate complex issues and come to difficult decisions. If the incidents in the case study on the TVEI submission had taken place at the end of a winter term how would the staff have coped with the meetings, the reading and the visits? (pp.137-40).

Some teachers may be unwilling to involve themselves in the

participative process. They take the view that they are employed to teach, and those who receive higher salaries are paid to take decisions. Those teachers who thus opt out may constitute a dissident group, alienated from the decisions of the majority. In other cases, disaffection may arise from a belief that, in spite of appearances, the system is manipulative rather than democratic. Not all teachers see the politics of the school as a fascinating or necessary part of their professional lives.

Some, while sympathetic to this democratic style of management, claim that teachers are resistant to change and that to seek consensus in such circumstances will lead to the adoption of a conservative approach. When vested interests are being threatened there may be a search for compromise and a reluctance to take radical decisions. If only easy issues can be dealt with by participation there will be a loss of confidence in the system, particularly if the difficult decisions are then taken albeit reluctantly by the senior management. The temptation for this to happen is illustrated clearly in the case study referred to above (p.137-40).

Summary

The present period is one of great changes, many of which seek to influence schools. There is a temptation in these circumstances to let those who are paid higher salaries make the decisions and then take the brickbats. Current pressures caused by the pace, centralised nature and resourcing pattern of changes are likely to reinforce this authoritarian mode of management.

However, we have taken the stance that teachers have a legitimate professional perspective on what is good for the children they teach and what constitutes worthwhile learning. A system which imposes decisions on schools to be implemented by managerial dictat or with minimal consultation is inimical to this view. A management style which orders, imposes, demands and instructs is at variance with an educational approach which stresses learning rather than instruction and which encourages discovery, development, negotiation and enquiry. Schools run as autocracies which treat teachers and pupils as a compliant work force cannot be expected to be healthy organisations in which to develop collaborative learning, cooperation or an understanding of democratic ways of thinking and behaving. Staff who take orders will tend to give orders. Staff who join in making decisions will tend to expect their students to do likewise. We question

whether an authoritarian school, run on a factory model aiming to
turn out a product which fits neatly into the national economy, really
has a place in a society that is undergoing profound changes such as
those of the information revolution, new patterns of employment, a
multi-ethnic society and threats to the global environment. Schools
cannot expect to remain isolated from these powerful influences and
will find themselves increasingly the subjects of intense public interest
and critical scrutiny. Changes are inevitable but if teachers are not to
be buffeted by every gust of change or harassed by conflicting
demands for change which are strident and often contradictory they
need strategies to plan change, and to maintain stability. To this end
we have presented a case for managing schools which unites teachers
as managers of learning in an organisation which is appropriate for
schools and in which they can share in determining the future of
young people. The style of management is supportive and the style of
leadership is creative.

Suggestions for further reading

HANDY, C. and AITKEN, R. (1986) *Understanding Schools as
    Organisations* (London, Penguin).
FULLAN, M. (1982) *The Meaning of Educational Change* (Toronto,
    OISE).
JOHN, D. (1980) *Leadership in Schools* (London, Heinemann).
SCHMUCK, R. A. (1981) *A Summary of School-Based Change
    Strategies. The State of the Art* (Oslo, IMTEC).

References

DES (1983) *Curriculum 11 to 16; Towards a Statement of Entitlement.
    Curriculum Re-Appraisal in Action* (HMSO).
HANDY, C. B. (1985) *Taken for Granted. Understanding Schools as
    Organisations* (London, Longman).
LIKERT, R. (1967) *The Human Organisation. Its Management and
    Value)* (Maidenhead, McGraw-Hill).
LIKERT, R. and LIKERT, J.G. (1976) *New Ways of Managing
    Conflict* (Maidenhead, McGraw-Hill).
MCGREGOR, D. (1960) *The Human Side of Enterprise* (Maidenhead,
    McGraw-Hill).

MACGREGOR-BURNS, J. (1978) *Leadership* (London, Harper and Row).

PETERS, T.J. and WATERMAN, R. H. J. (1983) *In Search of Excellence* (London, Harper and Row).

RUTTER, M. *et al* (1979) *Fifteen Thousand Hours* (London, Open Books).

TANNENBAUM, A. S. (1968) *Control in Organisations* (Maidenhead, McGraw-Hill).